PENGUIN BOOKS

REWRITE THE RULES

Ritu G. Mehrish has spent twenty years in the corporate world, working for P&G, GE Capital, and GE Spin off Genpact across the globe. In her last role she managed a multi-million-dollar business vertical with 1000 people across five continents. For the last ten years, she's been running her own consulting and coaching firm The Leadership Troubleshooter, which specializes in helping leaders and teams build sustainable leadership. Ritu has had the privilege of working with C-suite leaders from over thirty countries as a leadership coach and facilitator.

Ritu has a knack for identifying gaps in leadership narratives and bridging them through her research and work. Her previous book *Leader's Block: How great leaders recover after they stumble* normalized the fact that all leaders stumble in their career.

She is now empowering the next generation of women leaders by helping them get access to relatable role models.

Rajita, a seasoned leader with more than twenty-five years of experience—nineteen of which were spent at Google leading global learning & development—brings a diverse background in advertising, sales, and people development. Across leadership roles, she built high-performing teams, fostering the potential in others as a Level 5 leader.

Rajita facilitates programs in people management, leadership, and DE&I. As a certified coach, she empowers managers, individuals, and entrepreneurs. A doctor by training, Rajita's passions for Indian music and yoga influence her coaching, guiding clients to reach their full potential. She believes every aspect of life is interconnected, and everyone has the ability to excel.

Rajita continues to empower individuals and organizations through her own practice that is focused on coaching, learning and development, and well-being.

Together they host a highly popular podcast—*ReWrite The Rules*, where they interview seasoned women leaders across Asia.

ReWrite the Rules

How Women Leaders in Asia Are Changing the Leadership Paradigm

By

Ritu G. Mehrish
with
Rajita Saxena

PENGUIN BOOKS

An imprint of Penguin Random House

PENGUIN BOOKS

Penguin Books is an imprint of the Penguin Random House group of companies
whose addresses can be found at global.penguinrandomhouse.com

Published by Penguin Random House SEA Pte Ltd
40 Penjuru Lane, #03-12, Block 2
Singapore 609216

First published in Penguin Books by Penguin Random House SEA 2024

ISBN 9789815204674

Typeset in Yu Mincho, Yu Gothic Light by MAP Systems, Bengaluru, India
Printed at Repro India Limited

www.penguin.sg

Table of Contents

- Reflections and advice to one's younger self from various leaders: Timeless wisdom, personal anecdotes, and encouraging messages to inspire and guide the next generation of women leaders.

Preface

ReWrite the Rules is not just a title; it's a call to action.

We want to rewrite the 'standard operating procedures' of leadership, and we want to do it with you. And here is why:

- From observing history and reflecting on our own experience, we've learnt that clinging to outdated norms in a rapidly evolving world won't get us where we want to go.
- The current rules of leadership were written from a mostly western and mostly male perspective, and they don't address the unique challenges and advantages of being a woman leader in Asia.
- The voices of remarkable women leaders in Asia are not being heard and amplified enough. Even though they are making an impact, their work is lacking visibility. As a result, emerging women leaders in Asia are not able to find relatable role models.

We want to change these scenarios.

We want to address the gap that most women's leadership books overlook—the impact of cultural and societal norms that are unique to Asia. For example, women being the primary caregiver, the male-female gender stereotypes, male-dominated workplaces and leadership styles to name a few.

Asia is more than a geographic entity; it's a milieu of diverse cultures, burgeoning economies, and transformative businesses. Within this, women are increasingly stepping into leadership roles, bringing with them a fresh perspective on management, innovation, and societal impact. But in order for them to be successful, they require a more inclusive and conducive ecosystem in the form of role models, allies, and supportive organizations.

Our goal with *ReWrite the Rules* is to offer a first-hand nuanced look into the experiences, challenges, and successes of women leaders in Asia. We want this book to be a manual for change, and an action-oriented guide for women to step into the leadership roles they desire and deserve.

If you are a woman who grew up in Asia or spent a considerable amount of time in Asia navigating and embracing the unique gender challenges that this part of the world brings, then this is a book for you.

The book will help you navigate your leadership journey by rewriting your own rules of confidence, visibility, connection, balance, and growth. Given that every meaningful journey of growth starts with understanding ourselves better, this book will help you to reflect, understand, and assess your own leadership journey so far and identify your strengths and areas of focus.

Come along as we unpack the lives, challenges, and triumphs of women leaders who are rewriting the rules of leadership in Asia.

We invite you to join us as we, together, question, rethink, and rewrite the rules of leadership!

Introduction

I was gearing up for an important meeting with my CEO along with my boss. It was a cross functional strategy meeting with the company's leadership. I was excited and a bit nervous because I was the only woman leader and the first Asian women leader to be leading that meeting. To calm my nerves, I focused on my preparation and the insights I was about to bring to the table.

As I entered the room with my boss, Christian, a startling question came my way. A senior leader looked at me and asked, 'Are you the PA to Christian? Can you organize some coffee for the room?' I paused and was a bit taken aback but with a hint of humour, I responded, 'Nope, I'm the vice president of the strategy department, and I'm leading this meeting today!'

This is not a scene from the 50s, 60s, 70s, or 90s corporate world, this is from the year 2022. This is the story of a woman leader we interviewed for our book.

It's so hard to believe that in spite of so much talk about equality, equity, diversity, and inclusion in the last twenty years these biases still exist in the workplace. These instances also serve as a reminder that there is so much work that still needs to be done. They are proof that stereotypes and assumptions about gender normative roles—especially in leadership positions—continue to persist. And it's precisely these challenges that makes the journey of rewriting the rules of leadership so crucial for women leaders in Asia.

As Asian women leaders with experience in global corporations, we've witnessed first-hand the power of a supportive environment in fostering successful careers. We've also had the privilege of working alongside many inspiring Asian women who defied challenges and biases to build incredible careers. Their stories deserve to be heard!

This book is a culmination of our conversations with these remarkable Asian leaders who shattered glass ceilings and carved their own paths. Their experiences are not only inspiring, but also relatable—they are the role models that the next generation of Asian women leaders' needs.

↔

Ritu spent twenty years in the corporate world, working for P&G, GE Capital, and GE Spin off Genpact before starting her own consulting and coaching business. Ritu has worked in India, US, and Singapore, and over the last ten years, she has had the privilege of working closely with women leaders across Asia as a leadership coach and facilitator. Her consulting firm, The Leadership Troubleshooter, specializes in helping leaders and teams build sustainable leadership.

She has a knack for identifying gaps in leadership narratives and bridging them through her research and work. Her previous book *Leader's Block* normalized the fact that all leaders stumble in their career.

But there is something more personal that fuels her passion on the subject of this book.

Let's go back to the year 1971 in a small town in Uttar Pradesh, India. A young couple was sitting at a restaurant sipping their tea. A bunch of schoolgirls came in and sat on the table adjacent to them. The girls were busy giggling and talking to each other. The young woman was curious to hear what they were saying but she couldn't understand anything as they were talking in a language she didn't understand—English. She turned to her husband and said, 'When we have kids, I want them to speak like these girls.' Her husband smiled and nodded in agreement. In India, like most of Asia, speaking in English equals good education.

Flash forward fifty years, Ritu is one of the daughters of that visionary young lady. She and her siblings are a living testament to her foresight. Her mother defied the expectations of her time and rewrote the rules by aspiring for good quality education for her children.

This is not a mere anecdote. For Ritu, this has been the guiding factor in her life. It's a reminder that change often starts with a single decision, a single moment of clarity. In her mother's case, that one decision changed the trajectory of her family's future.

↔

Rajita began her career as a medical doctor and ran her own private practice for some time. A defining moment in her career was when she was approached by a friend to work for a startup in the training and development space. The excitement of learning something new, the joy of working in teams, and seeing the impact her work was having in shaping other people's career made the decision of eventually giving up private practice easy for her. She felt that she had found her calling. The only nagging feeling she had was that this would mean spending less time with her one-year-old daughter. But she was willing to try balancing both acts.

She didn't know then, but by defying the norm of being a practising physician, she rewrote the rules of defining growth and success for herself.

Adjusting to working in the corporate world wasn't easy for her. She had to build her knowledge and skills from scratch given that she hadn't formally studied business management. She read a lot of books and articles on management and boosted her subject matter expertise on the job. She credits the confidence she gained to adjust to a corporate culture of making presentations, working with others, and showcasing results to her mentor whose guidance and feedback were critical. Even today, she continues to be in touch with him.

Over the last twenty-five years, Rajita has been in several leadership and people management roles. She has led and managed sales, sales support, strategic operations, and learning and development teams. She has worked in India and Singapore and has rewritten several rules to grow her career in various disciplines. In keeping with her growth mindset, Rajita continued to learn and hone her skills both at work and in other areas by investing in becoming a learning and development programme facilitator, a coach, and a yoga teacher. She believes that it's the synergy between her various artistic pursuits and her corporate role that helps her be a better leader.

↔

We met in Singapore in 2016, and instantly connected over common interests and topics—one of them being a woman leader in the Asian context. The pandemic gave us a lot of time and space to think about leadership challenges for women in Asia. We felt that the landscape of leadership, especially when it came to women, often appeared lopsided. Though there are a lot of changes being made to corporate cultures to support women leaders, we found a gap that particularly impacts Asian women leaders.

A majority of the resources, research, books, corporate programmes, and case studies on women leadership are written through the Western lens. We found fewer insights that capture the full spectrum of leadership experiences that are unique to women leaders in Asia. Their stories, their challenges, and their triumphs are not spoken of and shared enough, and yet, these play a very crucial role in shaping their careers.

Finally in 2023, over a coffee conversation, we decided to come together as authors for *ReWrite the Rules*.

Why is it important to talk about women leadership in Asia? Let's put that into perspective through numbers.

Asia is home to nearly 60 per cent of the world's population. It holds a vital position in the global economic and social landscape, and a region that the rest of the world is watching closely as it is touted to be the primary driver of global economic growth in recent decades.

According to the McKinsey report '*The power of parity: Advancing women's equality in Asia Pacific*', countries could add $4.5 trillion to their collective GDP annually in 2025—a 12 per cent increase over a business-as-usual GDP trajectory. The same article also highlights that, 'In Asia Pacific, there is only one woman in leadership positions for every four men.' This is an average across Asia Pacific countries with some countries having a worse representation of women leaders than others.

Additionally, in their report titled '*How advancing women's equality can add $12 trillion to global growth*', McKinsey Global Institute (MGI), an independent, global research and analysis company, established a strong link between gender equality in work and in society. As per their report, gender equality in workplace is not achievable without gender equality in society at large. Gender inequality overall has a negative impact on economic growth of a country.

This makes it absolutely vital to recognize the importance of women in Asia's workforce, invest in their growth, and support them to navigate the unique challenges they face both within and outside the business arena. This will lead to fewer women dropping out of the workforce, and more women representation in leadership positions. It makes smart business sense to invest in women not just to address gender disparities but tap into the full potential of the region's talent pool for sustained growth and innovation. By investing in women leaders, we are investing in the future of Asia.

We wrote this book as an invitation to our fellow Asian women leaders to challenge the old rules that have threatened to restrict our growth and to rewrite these rules to make them work for us and those that come after us.

Throughout the book, you'll see the names of real women leaders and hear how they've navigated the very terrain you're on. They've scaled the peaks, overcome the hurdles, and left a trail of wisdom that you can leverage to fast-track your own success.

These are women leaders who have either successfully navigated careers in traditional male-dominated fields or have transitioned from one discipline to another, entirely pivoting their careers. Then there are some who have struck the delicate balance between personal and professional lives, and others who have redefined the definition of growth.

To emphasize on some key learnings, we've also created hypothetical stories where, while the characters are not real, the scenarios they are in are relatable.

Our focus is not on identifying the problems because a lot has already been said, and neither is it on blaming others. *ReWrite the Rules* urges you to stop waiting for permission or fitting some predefined stereotype. It's about taking charge, embracing your power, and defining success on your own terms.

While the world of leadership is vast and multifaceted, this book focuses primarily on women in the corporate workforce. Women across all levels—from emerging professionals to senior women leaders—can expect to find pointers that can help them thrive in their careers.

To ensure we are capturing the diverse voices of women leaders across the region, we took inputs from over 500 women leaders. We engaged in extensive dialogue with over 200 women leaders from various levels, backgrounds, and industry experience. These women represent a broad range of the corporate world, entrepreneurship, social enterprise, academia, and even sports. They come from different parts of Asia: Singapore, Malaysia, India, Thailand, China, the Philippines, Indonesia, Japan, Vietnam, and beyond.

To further strengthen our understanding, we surveyed over 200 women leaders to gather their insights and perspectives. We also spoke with male allies—individuals who have played pivotal roles in supporting and championing women leaders.

Based on all these interviews, conversations, and data, we've identified five core areas to dive into—feeling confident, building networks, creating visibility, achieving balance, and defining success. These core areas form the crux of the book, and we've also spoken about the importance of allyship.

We have kept the book pragmatic in its approach. We will be exploring the traditional rules of leadership with a lens to what is relevant (or not) to women leaders in Asia today and which rules need to be entirely rewritten. Each chapter has real life stories of leaders just like you, guidance on rewriting the rules, actionable solutions, and strategies that you can implement as you navigate your own journey. At the end of each chapter there is an opportunity for you to pause, reflect, and assess the various aspects of your career, and take action to create a customized plan for yourself. The book can be read sequentially, or you can jump right into a chapter that piques your interest.

We are certain of one thing—the approach described in the book about rewriting the rules is such that it will work for you and help you reach your full potential and make you the best version of yourself.

What it does require though is the courage to accept what needs to change, the willingness to take charge of one's career, and own the responsibility to see the change through to the end.

Through this book we are bringing our stories, experiences, and optimism to you, and we hope that the book becomes your guide in your leadership journey.

Remember, this is not just a book. It's a call to take control, rewrite the rules, and make your mark!

Let's dive in!

1

The Being Confident Rule

Fresh out of school, I was an accountant, primed for the typical path—a few years at a Big Four firm followed by a corporate climb. Landing a job at a Dutch manufacturing company in Singapore, and then moving to Seagate, I started as a cost accountant in the factory.

Seagate, with its diverse operations, offered opportunities beyond traditional accounting. I transitioned from finance to pricing, then product line management, and eventually to Business Development (BD) sales. Sales enablement, my current role, was a path I never envisioned.

The turning point in my career was a manager who truly shaped me. Early in my career, when I was hesitant about a US assignment, he encouraged me to take the leap. This experience exposed me to a new world— different work styles, a culture of open communication, and the confidence to speak up in meetings.

In Asia, junior employees traditionally remain silent in meetings dominated by senior figures. In the US, I learned to contribute and make my voice and my ideas heard. This shift was crucial—not just for feedback, but for developing the confidence to know I was on the right track.

Being a woman in a male-dominated industry presented challenges. Twenty years ago, in a company dominated by engineers and men, I was often the only woman at the table. While some voices were heard, there was a hesitancy to contribute for fear of not being supported. Thankfully, diversity awareness has grown significantly in recent years, creating a more inclusive environment where women's voices can be heard.

Early in my career, I felt most comfortable with numbers and finance, my area of expertise. Sales presentations and pitches were intimidating. However, a sales manager I worked closely with encouraged me to step outside my comfort zone and take on a sales role. This was the biggest risk I'd ever taken—transitioning from an internal to an external facing role.

Looking back, that decision was instrumental in getting me where I am today. The role involved developing emerging markets, a critical area of growth for the company. Taking on the challenge, I grew the revenue from $850 million to $1.2 billion within four years. By the time I left, it was one of the company's most profitable businesses.

The success of this role stemmed largely from the coaching of my exceptional manager. He was a natural salesperson who emphasized a balanced approach—advocating for the company while building strong relationships. Coming from finance, my focus was often on protecting the company. This role, however, required developing soft skills to build partnerships and a strong sales team, a stark contrast to the finance DNA I possessed.

The unwavering support and coaching from my manager instilled the confidence and skills that have enabled me to achieve success in my career. It was a journey of unexpected turns, but one that has led me to a place of fulfilment and accomplishment.

This story was shared by LayPeng Ong, vice president of Global Sales Operations and Enablement at Seagate Technology, Singapore. LayPeng grew up in Singapore and went on to study in the US before coming back to Singapore to begin her corporate career with Seagate Technologies.

↔

Decoding Confidence

Confidence is a powerful word. It is more about a feeling than an external characteristic. It's a belief in oneself, one's abilities, and that mental and emotional state that allows us to feel capable of handling whatever challenges come our way. It is about having a realistic sense of our strengths and weaknesses. It doesn't mean that you think you are perfect!

When we looked further into the definition and understanding of confidence across multiple disciplines, including psychology, business, and social sciences, we saw that there isn't one single definition. Confidence is often presented as a multi-dimensional construct. It includes various interdependent factors like the belief in one's ability to succeed in a particular situation, the overall evaluation of one's self-worth, the ability to understand one's own strengths, weaknesses, and emotions, the ability to interact with others in a positive and assertive way, and the ability to manage one's emotions in a healthy way.

As we dug deeper in our research, we came across other interesting dimensions of confidence that are not spoken a lot about—epistemic confidence and social confidence.

Epistemic Confidence

This type of confidence is about your belief in your own knowledge and intellectual capabilities. It's the confidence you feel when you're sure you know the answer to a question, you can solve a problem, or can complete a task that requires a certain level of expertise. It's the feeling you get when you're well-prepared for a meeting or when you're speaking about a subject you've deeply researched.

Epistemic confidence is built through education, experience, and competence. When a subject matter expert like a software engineer or an accountant has acquired deep knowledge in their respective fields, that knowledge helps them meet their objectives and goals. This type of knowledge building exemplifies epistemic confidence.

To continue to strengthen this type of confidence, you need to:

Know your strengths and leverage them

- Spend time to reflect on and understand the things you do well and develop ways to integrate them into daily life.

Track your successes

- Keep a list of all your accomplishments, skills, achievements, and contributions that you can look back on to boost your confidence, and update that list regularly. This will not only boost your confidence but also prepare you to articulate your value to the organization.

Continue to upskill

- Spend time to enhance your expertise in your chosen field of expertise. This could involve pursuing advanced degrees, participating in relevant workshops, or engaging with the latest research in your field. As your expertise grows, so will your self-assuredness in tackling challenges.

Most women we work with are high on epistemic confidence. They have invested time and effort in building expertise and rely on the knowledge they've gained to help them navigate situations in their career.

And that's a great start!

However, we've noticed many women stumble because they are not cautious of some blind spots associated with relying too heavily on your knowledge. For instance, relying too much on mastering the content of a presentation rather than practising its delivery or preparing for the questions that might come up. Therefore, while it's great to have an open-minded approach to new information and knowledge, be careful so you don't become overly reliant on only what you've learned. In addition, always challenge your assumptions and seek different perspectives to get a holistic view of a situation rather than depending on your knowledge alone.

Social Confidence

Social confidence is your ability to navigate social situations effectively. It's the sense of ease and comfort you feel in social situations and work settings like meetings, while giving a presentation, or networking at a business event.

Having the confidence to raise your hand to ask a question in the town hall, making a different point of view in a meeting, or reaching out to others for feedback are some other examples of social confidence.

Unlike epistemic confidence, which focuses on the knowledge you possess, social confidence is more about your ability to effectively interact with others, communicate your ideas, and build meaningful relationships.

Social confidence is heavily influenced by cultural factors like social norms, social expectations, and role models. This is more so for women than men as women navigate additional gendered stereotypes in interactions; like the idea that we are soft-spoken, accommodating, and not keen on voicing our opinion. There is research that also examines how confidence is perceived and manifested differently across cultures. For instance, studies have found that people from individualistic cultures, such as US and Canada, tend to be more confident in their abilities than people from collectivistic cultures, as seen in many Asian countries.

The studies suggest that this difference is due to the difference in values that are emphasized in these cultures. In individualistic cultures, people are encouraged to be independent and self-reliant, while in collectivistic cultures, people are encouraged to be modest and humble. Therefore, women from individualistic cultures are more likely to be confident in their abilities than women in collectivistic cultures.

While cultural shifts and changing norms are beginning to help improve women's social confidence, one quick start that women can make to enhance their social confidence is to eliminate self-deprecating language.

Very often women will purposely soften their statements in order to not come off as direct, harsh, or arrogant. They will say things like, 'I'm no expert, but . . .' or 'I'm sorry, but . . .' What they don't realize is that instead of coming across as modest, they come across as under-confident and unsure of themselves.

Stopping this negative talk will help you come off in a better light, even if you are unsure, and it'll sure make you feel better about yourself and improve your self-confidence.

In conversations with several women leaders, we found that when they say, 'I don't feel confident,' most often they are referring to social confidence. However, there can be a tendency to over invest in epistemic confidence as a way to build confidence overall and not give enough attention to social confidence.

In the context of women leaders, defining confidence or discussing confidence becomes complex due to the interplay of gender dynamics, societal expectations, and differing workplace cultures.

In the business world both are important; the key is to find that balance.

But before we dive into it, let us take you to the year 2000 to share a personal story.

Ritu's Story

I moved to work in the US in the early 2000 as part of my job with GE Capital Consumer Finance. I was part of the regulatory reporting team which was a small but very critical group that reported GE's financial numbers to the Federal Reserve Bank. At the end of every quarter, we had to present the numbers to all the key business leaders before submitting them.

I was responsible for preparing the financial reports and writing the commentary. Once I had the reports ready, my manager, Don, would review them, and then present them to the business leaders. Quarter after quarter, I watched, in awe of how confidently Don presented and answered all the questions that the business leaders would have.

After a year, Don said, 'Ritu, you are doing a great job! I would like you to present the financials next quarter.' I wasn't prepared for it because I could never imagine myself speaking in front of that senior an audience. I had no confidence in myself and was acutely aware of the difference in the way I spoke, and in the way I looked, and that was too daunting for me.

I tried to wriggle out of it but then Don sensed my reluctance and started to nudge me. Realizing I could not avoid it any further, I gave in to the nudging and started to prepare for the presentation. I wrote detailed notes, pre-empted every question and wrote their answers. When the day came, I was super nervous but kept a calm exterior and managed to do an okay job. I felt that I wasn't brilliant. Don had to step in multiple times to respond to questions from the audience. However, the act of leading the conversation built a little confidence in me. This continued for a few quarters, and one day Don asked me how I felt. I sheepishly told him, 'I feel very self-conscious as I have a different accent, different skin tone, and different gender when compared to all the attendees.' This was because I was Indian, and I was the only woman in that room.

That day Don said something that has stayed with me always. He asked me, 'Ritu, do you know why there is complete silence when you speak?' I jokingly said maybe they don't get what I say due to my accent. He said, 'No, they listen because you know your stuff so well, and you provide a different perspective. And, of course, you sound different. But that difference is your superpower, and you should always leverage that!'

That conversation shaped my thinking for years to come. When I look back, I believe that had it not been for Don, I would have struggled to find that confidence in my abilities, or I would have tried hard to feel confident through superficial factors like modifying my accent, dressing up differently, acting differently to fit in, and thus losing my authenticity in the bargain.

Over the following years, these two things became my mantra of feeling confident:

Always put in the work and prepare well for all interactions—big or small

- We often spend time preparing before a big presentation but what about preparing for a meeting with your team, or for the one on one with your manager? Whatever the stakes in a meeting, preparing well for it goes a long way. This shows that working on building expertise and mastering your topic (epistemic confidence) can really make you feel confident.

Leverage your difference

- Don't try to be like everyone else as that will not be sustainable and, on the contrary, it will probably be exhausting. Identify the style that works for you and recognize what makes you feel comfortable in your skin. Ask for feedback from people who are invested in your success because they can highlight your strengths and your blind spots. Embrace this feedback and be comfortable with who you are in the moment (social confidence).

In my case, I noticed that when I moved to the US, I was initially very reluctant to speak in meetings due to my accent, but that conversation with Don changed my whole perspective. My belief was further strengthened during my work in Europe where I noticed that most Europeans are not native English speakers and they spoke English with differing proficiency and different accents—and they had no qualms about it!

↔

Continuing our conversation on social confidence, from our research and several conversations with women leaders, we recognize that the basic tenets of confidence—the belief in one's abilities and skills coupled with a willingness to take action remain the same for men and women. However, there are unique challenges and considerations for women, especially in an Asian setting given the added layer of cultural expectations. Here are some of the common ones:

Double standards

- Women leaders sometimes find themselves in a situation where displaying confidence can be misinterpreted as arrogance or being 'too aggressive'. Whereas similar behaviour from a man is viewed as a positive and expected behaviour. Women often fear that being in the limelight will expose them to more criticism. Women leaders may be concerned that any flaws or mistakes will be magnified and used to undermine their competence and credibility.

Cultural expectations

- Asian cultures often prize modesty and humility which are in conflict with the Western idea of what confident behaviour looks like (e.g. assertiveness, direct communication). From a young age, women have been told subtly and overtly that they should be humble, accommodating, and not draw too much attention to themselves. We carry forward some of these notions into our adulthood. Therefore, women leaders sometimes find it difficult to display confidence openly because it may be interpreted as challenging senior authority figures, especially in male-dominated industries.

Nuances of identity

- Navigating professional spaces as a woman leader in Asia becomes more intricate when considering the intersection of factors like ethnicity, social class, and even regional differences. For instance, language barriers when trying to communicate effectively in the dominant language of the workplace or certain industries might be more male-dominated in some regions compared to others. These interwoven identities can shape how women leaders approach and navigate professional settings like in Ritu's case.

Gendered confidence gap

- Various studies have shown that women on average rate their abilities lower than men do, even when their performance does not differ significantly. 'Advancing the Future of Women in Business: A KPMG Women's Leadership Summit Report' polled 750 high-performing executive women who are one or two career steps away from the C-suite. One of the key findings of the report was that 75 per cent of women leaders experience imposter syndrome despite their accomplishments.

Communication styles

- Women leaders display confidence differently and use more collaborative language or seek consensus. While this is not 'lesser' confidence, in corporate settings, this type of behaviour is often equated with not being assertive.

Language

Before we move on, we want to take a moment to talk about language. Fluency in the English language plays a big part in displaying confidence through communication, especially for women leaders in Asia who are working in multinational corporate English-speaking environments.

Most Asians are not native English speakers, and they often find themselves pulling back or not sharing their thoughts openly in a multinational workforce environment. This could be due to the lack of comfort or confidence in speaking English, and that can come across as lack of confidence.

In Asia, where English is often the second language for many professionals, these challenges and strategies take on special relevance especially in multinational, international organizations where English is the primary business language. Understanding the dynamics of language and confidence can be crucial for both individual leaders and organizations.

It's an area that we have seen up close through our women leadership programmes and as non-native English speakers ourselves.

Here is how we've seen the lack of comfort with communicating in English manifest itself negatively in a workplace and impact social confidence:

Fear of Mistakes

- An exaggerated concern about making grammatical errors and having a distinct non-native English accent can lead to hesitancy in speaking up, thereby affecting overall confidence.

Cultural Nuances

- Idioms, humour, and colloquialisms can be hard to grasp for non-native speakers, and this might lead to feelings of inadequacy or exclusion.

Limited Vocabulary

- A more limited vocabulary can sometimes restrict the ability to express complex thoughts or concepts or engage in critical conversations that then might affect self-esteem in professional settings.

Group Dynamics

- In meetings or group discussions, not being fluent in English could result in reticence to engage, that in turn leads to lower visibility and perceived lack of confidence.

Self-Perpetuating Cycle

Through our research, as we spoke to more women leaders on the topic of confidence, we saw a pattern emerge that we are calling the 'self-perpetuating cycle' (see *Figure 1*).

The behaviour that often begins due to societal norms and expectations ends up self-perpetuating within the workplace as well.

Often, as women leaders, we've seen that most of us have the tendency to shy away from the limelight in professional settings. If women are less likely to step into the limelight or ask for visible roles due to social conditioning, fear of judgement, etc., it's very likely that they can be overlooked when career opportunities arise.

This is because people may wrongly assume that the women in the organization are not interested in or capable of such roles. So, the roles go to men, and women continue to not ask for what they want, thereby reinforcing the cycle and creating a self-fulfilling prophecy.

Self-Perpetuating Cycle

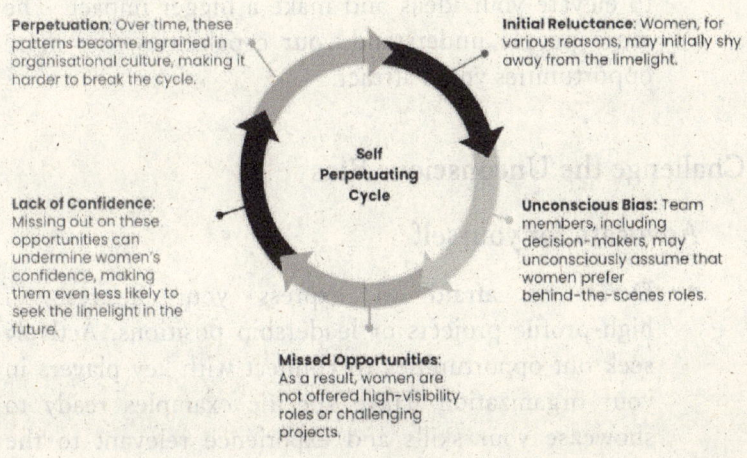

Figure 1

We can all relate to this as it's happened to all of us at some time. We see it so often in organizations, and this cycle impacts how confidence manifests itself and is displayed by women in leadership settings and roles. We hear a version of it in our conversations with male colleagues too.

This cycle can be broken, but it requires concerted effort from both organizations and individuals. That said, there are concrete steps that women, too, can take at an individual level to actively disrupt this pattern.

Reframe the Limelight

Practice self-promotion

- Instead of waiting to be recognized, find comfortable ways to showcase your accomplishments. This could involve creating presentations on projects you led, volunteering for speaking engagements, or writing articles highlighting your expertise.

Shift the spotlight

- View visibility not as self-promotion, but as a chance to elevate your ideas and make a bigger impact. The more people understand your capabilities, the more opportunities you'll attract.

Challenge the Unconscious Bias

Advocate for yourself

- Don't be afraid to express your interest in high-profile projects or leadership positions. Actively seek out opportunities to connect with key players in your organization. Have specific examples ready to showcase your skills and experience relevant to the opportunity.

Address the bias head-on

- If you suspect unconscious bias is holding you back, have a candid conversation with a trusted mentor or colleague. Together, you can strategize ways to overcome these barriers.

Be Proactive

Highlight your transferable skills

- Even if a project doesn't directly align with your current expertise, focus on the transferable skills you can bring to the table. Show your willingness to learn and grow in new areas.

Build a reputation for excellence

- Consistently deliver high-quality work and demonstrate your ability to handle complex tasks. This will make you a go-to person for important assignments.

Cultivate Confidence

Focus on your strengths

- Make a list of your skills and accomplishments. Reminding yourself of your capabilities can combat self-doubt and increase your confidence.

Find a mentor

- Having a mentor who believes in you can be invaluable. They can provide guidance, support, and honest feedback to help you build your confidence.

Break the Missed Opportunity Pattern

Celebrate your successes

- Take the time to acknowledge your achievements, no matter how small. This reinforces your confidence and motivates you to continue pushing forward.

Seek inspiration

- Look for role models who have successfully broken the cycle. Their stories can provide valuable inspiration and guidance.

Remember, breaking this cycle takes time and effort. Be patient with yourself, celebrate your progress, and don't be afraid to ask for help to develop your confidence.

↔

Rajita's Story

A few days after being promoted into a new role, I was going to be making an important presentation. I was really excited and looking forward to sharing my understanding of business insights.

However, I was quite perplexed when my manager pinged me over chat the next day after the presentation and gave me very abrupt feedback that I needed to improve my business acumen. This feedback was given to me over chat with no context, no examples of where I can improve, or what I did wrong. Despite multiple follow ups, I didn't receive any guidance from my manager. They showed no ownership of the feedback and neither did they offer any constructive suggestions to help me improve.

From being self-assured and on a high from my recent promotion, my confidence took a bad hit. I spent days ruminating on how I could go so wrong. I played the presentation meeting multiple times in my head trying to understand what I missed. My anxiety was heightened, and my self-esteem was at an all-time low.

It took me a few months to overcome the initial feeling of doom, and in a conversation with a close friend at work, I realized that I could take control of the situation, and more importantly, of my emotions and reactions to the incident.

I started by revisiting the presentation I made, but this time from the perspective of learning rather than trying to figure out what went wrong. I spoke to several confidants as to where I could have done better. I read up and learned from other experts about the business and spent a lot of time shadowing my team to understand the nuts and bolts of the work we did. This really helped me rebuild my confidence as I slowly built my expertise.

The next thing I did was to start talking about the work, share my perspective, and voice my opinion in forums that mattered. I would sign up for meetings with senior leaders in the team and share my thoughts on the business. By sharing my point of view and seeking feedback from peers and seniors, I slowly garnered confidence in myself as the response to my perspective grew positive.

I grew bolder and was slowly able to showcase my unique knowledge and experience as it influenced my understanding of the business differently.

It took me months to overcome this setback. However, at the end of it, I learned that it's important to understand that you can only control what is controllable. For instance, instead of blaming the manager, I eventually tried to figure out what I could do to change and influence how I show up as a leader in my organization. I took charge of my situation and worked to build my knowledge and reputation.

Today, anytime I have a setback, my confidence may take a dip. However, I know that I can work through any challenges if I focus on what I can do to influence a change.

↔

So far, we've discussed how confidence for women leaders is often defined and assessed similarly to men, but research clearly shows that it is shaped and often constrained by a variety of external and internal factors that don't impact men similarly. If women in Asia are to find confidence in their authentic selves, then these factors will require a nuanced and culturally sensitive approach to help foster confidence in women rather than just using the rules laid out by the Western world on what confidence means.

By outlining these challenges, we hope to normalize them so that the human resources, diversity, equity, and inclusion leaders and business leaders are more aware and acknowledge these unique challenges. Our hope is that this will guide an organization's leadership and talent development interventions differently by tailoring them to help women leaders overcome these challenges.

But like we said earlier, there is a role women can play in owning their experience and taking steps to build their own confidence. So, let's see how they can go about doing so.

↔

This is how Sasibai Kimis Steenland, who left a successful career in the finance industry to start the award-winning impact enterprise and craftsmanship focused brand, EARTH HEIR®, built confidence while building and growing the social enterprise ecosystem. She is currently based in Malaysia and was one of Wharton's 40 under 40 award winners in 2015 and an Eisenhower Fellow in the 2015 Women's Leadership Program.

This is the story of my journey, building a social enterprise in Malaysia as a woman and a minority. It's a story of challenges overcome, and lessons learned, all fuelled by a determination to make a positive impact.

My self-confidence plummeted when I left my corporate finance role and sought to start anew in the social impact space. In my financial career, I was used to a certain level of social standing, I suppose, but I was essentially a nobody in the social impact world when I started. However, while I was in the private equity and corporate finance worlds, where I was often the only woman in a room full of men, micro-aggressions such as sexist jokes and sometimes getting asked to get coffee, were fairly common. In the midst of this, women need to define their spaces and set our boundaries for behaviour.

Having to start from the bottom in the social impact space, I decided to build on my strengths, Wharton education, and experience in finance. While this was initially something I hesitated to leverage, they became assets. It gave me the credibility and the language to speak to those from the corporate sectors. I learned to use my background to advocate for social enterprises, a sector often seen as lacking street cred in the corporate world.

Starting out as a social impact entrepreneur, I found myself comparing myself to others—a trap that stifled my progress. I quickly learned this valuable lesson: Stay focused on your own lane. In 2024, after eleven years of steady growth, Earth Heir® is ready to take a bigger leap. We have started a sustainability and social impact centre and transformed EarthHeir.com into a social impact marketplace to empower others and create a positive ecosystem.

Looking back, my biggest learnings have been:

o   Don't be afraid or embarrassed to ask for help. There are many who may want to support you, they can't read your mind.

o   Avoid comparison traps. Focus on your own lane, don't look left or right and forget the purpose of why you started in the first place. If you can, try and not start a new business on your own. Having a strong support system and partners whom you can bounce ideas off is essential for your well-being and your venture's success.

↔

Place of Traditional Rules of Confidence in Today's World

From our research we found that, traditionally, the definition of confidence often aligns with certain behaviours and traits that are widely recognized and have stood the test of time. We saw that the following are things that people noticed when they said someone is confident:

Strong Posture

- Standing up straight with shoulders back, head held high, and maintaining steady eye contact is a universal sign of confidence. It signals self-assurance and engagement.

Direct and Clear Communication

- English is accepted as the common language for conducting international business. When a person generally speaks clearly, at a good pace, has a good command over English at the workplace, and avoids excessive jargon or filler words, they are perceived as more confident.

Controlled Gestures

- Using facial expressions and hand gestures for emphasis but taking care to not let them become frantic or excessive indicates control and confidence.

The next three are more subtle and become noticeable when you work with the person closely.

Decisive Action

- A confident person makes decisions and sticks to them. Indecision or constant flip-flopping is generally seen as a lack of confidence.

Risk-taking

- Being willing to take calculated risks after doing one's due diligence is traditionally seen as a sign of confidence.

Unflappability

- Maintaining composure in stressful or unexpected situations shows confidence in one's ability to cope with ambiguity and complexity.

This brings us to the question: Is displaying confidence more important than feeling confident?

We don't have the perfect answer. However, we do know that each one of us can find a balance that works for us.

REWRITE THE RULES

Be Yourself

Traditional markers of confidence are being augmented by new, innovative ways to display self-assurance and leadership. Based on our conversations with the leaders and our own experience of working with leaders, here are some ways women leaders are rewriting and can rewrite the rule of feeling confident.

Women leaders are now sharing their thought process, decision making, personal stories and experiences unabashedly. This can signify a new kind of confidence where authenticity is increasingly becoming a valued trait in modern corporate culture. If you combine showing up as your true self with being comfortable with who you are, you will have a winning combination.

In today's global work environment, we are constantly on virtual meetings and are very likely working with people across cultures, making it hard to imitate another person's style or try to modify our style to different people and cultures. Instead, focusing on being your authentic self on these virtual platforms is both an easier option and an essential component.

We learned from our conversations with women leaders that there is no one way to be authentic. Some women felt that dressing up helped them feel confident even in virtual meetings, and on the other hand we heard from some other women leaders that they felt confident even with the camera on to show up just as they are.

↔

Gloria Ngooi is HR director at Ikano Retail, IKEA. She is based in Singapore and has extensive experience in human resources in multiple retail industries. Gloria shared with us her approach to building confidence.

> Gloria advises young women leaders to be confident in themselves and not worry about conforming or having a different point of view.
>
> She says it's okay and valuable to voice out your own perspective, even if it differs from others. She mentioned that as one of the few women in a senior role, speaking up and having her voice heard in meetings can sometimes be challenging, and it was then that she realized that women shouldn't be afraid to speak up as a minority voice because if they didn't they would never be heard.
>
> Gloria emphasized that establishing relationships and credibility so colleagues respect and connect with you was important because it instils confidence in you that your voice will be heard when you speak up.
>
> On the role of criticism or feedback in building or breaking confidence, she suggested not dwelling on unhelpful criticism. Gloria says, 'Take it as input, make changes if it's valuable, and move on.' She talked about decluttering relationships and not dwelling on unhelpful criticism or perceptions, suggesting that confidence

comes from within rather than others' views, and that one should be basing confidence on internal measures rather than others' validation.

She encouraged taking on challenges, being courageous and contributing more than expected, implying confidence is built by taking calculated risks and expanding beyond one's comfort zone. Gloria said she gained confidence from her organization believing in her and providing opportunities to take on stretch roles. Having this institutional confidence helped build her self-assurance.

Gloria highlighted building self-assurance from within, speaking your truth, controlling reactions to feedback, and taking risks to gain confidence through experience as a way to continue to invest in building confidence. Her advice to her younger self is not to fear failure and to explore more, pointing to confidence coming from experience and learning from failures.

↔

While being proficient in English as a business language is important, being bilingual or multilingual can provide a unique cultural perspective that can be an asset in global business environments. For instance, if a multinational corporation has a project in an Asian country and you are proficient in the language, then you can be a bridge between the regional and central team because of your understanding of both sides.

We continue to leverage our understanding of Asia and working in global organizations to our advantage. Additionally, navigating multiple languages often requires a high degree of adaptability, a trait that itself exudes confidence. And experiencing language barriers can make one more empathetic toward others who face similar challenges, and empathy is often viewed as a leadership strength.

Expand Your Influence

The rise of remote work and digital platforms have provided an avenue for women leaders to create a strong online presence. Across the world, women from all walks of life are leveraging platforms to share thought leadership articles, podcast episodes about their journeys, corporate or otherwise, to display confidence in themselves and their achievements.

This is incumbent on learning and being confident with technology. Many women leaders are displaying confidence through their willingness to quickly learn and adapt to new technologies, methodologies, or industry trends. This shows confidence in one's ability to grow and adapt.

So, here are some things that you can do: Create your online presence, update your online job profiles, connect with like-minded professionals by joining a professional network, listen to people from your field to broaden your horizons, share your thoughts and perspectives with your professional groups, etc.

Don't wait for a high-visibility project to come your way, create your own opportunities to showcase your talents. For instance, if you're interested in a high-visibility project or a leadership role, make it known and explicitly express interest. Sometimes, saying it out loud is half the battle.

Remember, it is equally important to decline tasks that are not aligned with your career goals or are traditionally 'assigned' to women, like office housework or event planning, unless it's something you genuinely enjoy and find rewarding.

↔

Rachanee Chanawatr is a Principal Investment Officer at International Finance Corporation (IFC), World Bank Group. She comes with extensive experience of leading organizations in varied industries. However, she began her career as a dentist who then moved to working in corporate. She's currently based in Thailand. She shared with us how she overcame the issue of lacking confidence while stepping into new territories as she moved from one industry and role to another.

My career path has been anything but linear. It's a testament to the importance of embracing challenges and continuously building confidence.

The first, and perhaps biggest, confidence hurdle I faced was a complete career switch—from dentistry to business. Fresh out of business school, as a pathway switching from being a dentist, I lacked the confidence to fully commit to business. So, I kept my dentistry licence active and continued to practise over the weekend as a safety net in case things didn't work out. It took a few years to fully trust myself in this new path.

Throughout my career, building confidence has been a recurring theme. Each new role, industry, and territory brought a fresh set of challenges. It wasn't always easy, but I learned to leverage my transferable skills and focus on the bigger picture.

Fortunately, early on in my consulting career, I had a fantastic boss who believed in me. He empowered me with independence and authority, treating me more like a coach than a supervisor. He even entrusted me with a daunting first assignment—overseas negotiations with a major pharmaceutical company CFO. Looking back, that initial challenge, though nerve-wracking, became a springboard for developing my confidence and resilience.

Another key ingredient for my success has been a strong focus on teamwork. At every stage of my career, I've prioritized understanding the team's goals and leveraging the strengths of each member. This collaborative approach not only fosters a positive work environment but also boosts individual confidence by creating opportunities for growth and development.

Transitioning into leadership roles often meant navigating unfamiliar territory, feeling like an outsider. However, I've learned to overcome this by aligning myself with the team's goals and focusing on how I can contribute. This not only builds confidence but also fosters stronger team dynamics.

↔

Demonstrate Resilience and Agility

With all the disruption in the fields of health, technology, and geo-political systems, organizations are counting on leaders to have the ability to adapt to setbacks.

More women leaders are seen stepping up and displaying resilience-based confidence. Additionally, women leaders are known to encourage diverse opinions and create an environment where all voices are heard. These behaviours display the confidence of a leader who is secure enough to be challenged.

If you notice practices or policies that contribute to the self-perpetuating cycle, bring it up for discussion. Your perspective could be the catalyst for organizational change. By taking action, women can begin to break the cycle that keeps them out of high-visibility roles. It will not happen overnight, and it will require consistent effort, but every step taken is a move toward creating a more inclusive and equitable work environment.

↔

Here is what Dr Vinika D. Rao, one of the women leaders we spoke to, shared how she boosted her confidence by self-improvement, establishing trust, taking risks, and not tying self-worth tightly to external measures of achievement. Her story is a great example of resilience in building confidence. Dr Rao began her career with a multinational bank in India and is currently the executive director of INSEAD Africa Initiative and

Hoffmann Institute for Business & Society, Asia, and an adjunct professor at INSEAD and SMU. She also sits on several boards and advisory boards and advises organizations on DEI and ESG. Her research interests include gender diversity in corporate leadership, male allyship, millennials & multigenerational influences in the workplace, and emerging market strategies.

Like many other women leaders, I've battled imposter syndrome and with self-doubt about my abilities. Changing careers and landing senior roles amplified this feeling. As GM of an Industrial Chemicals company, I would sometimes wonder whether the chemical engineers around me took my MBA in Finance seriously. My bosses noticed my potential but urged me to be more assertive. Fortunately, I refused to let my own doubts define me and forced myself to own my accomplishments and project confidence. It wasn't easy, but with each step, I felt my self-belief grow.

Another key challenge was creating visibility for my achievements. I used to believe that good work would be recognized on its own. However, a friend pointed out a crucial truth: my efficiency, while impressive, made my hard work invisible. 'You make everything look easy,' he said. In my work with senior women leaders, I've seen that many of them face this dilemma. We quietly take on increased responsibility and deliver results, only to be overlooked.

This realization sparked a change. I learned to advocate for myself by strategically highlighting my accomplishments. It wasn't about self-promotion; it was about ensuring my contributions were acknowledged. It didn't come naturally; I did have to 'fake it till I made it' but it got easier.

What really helped me build my resilience has been my genuine interest in people, understanding what makes them tick and how we can collaborate for mutual benefit.

This has helped to build true connections without any conscious networking and created lasting professional association and personal friendship. These networks, formed organically through authentic conversations, became a source of support and a platform for further growth. This journey is far from over. But by embracing resilience, owning my worth, and building meaningful connections, I'm thriving in leadership roles like the countless impressive women leaders I work with.

↔

No One Way

There's no one approach for building confidence—it's a unique journey for everyone. The path you take will be shaped by your personality, cultural background, workplace environment, and even societal expectations. A strategy that propels one person forward might not resonate with another. The key is to discover what works best for you and leverage your strengths to cultivate a sense of self-assuredness.

↔

Let's look at the journey that Jacky and Lily, our two fictitious leaders, took to build and demonstrate their confidence.

SCENARIO

A high-stakes strategy meeting at QuantumTech Corp.

KEY PLAYERS

- **Jacky:** Director of sales at QuantumTech Corp, a fast-paced tech startup. Has a background in engineering and believes 'winning is everything'.

- **Lily:** Head of product development at QuantumTech Corp. Holds a Ph.D. in Computer Science and values collaboration and inclusivity.

BEFORE THE MEETING

Jacky walks into the conference room for the pre-meeting huddle, her shoulders squared, and head held high. She offers a handshake to everybody. 'Morning, team. Ready to crack this presentation?'

Lily enters the room. She smiles warmly at everyone, saying, 'Good morning! How's everyone feeling?'

DURING THE MEETING

Jacky kicks off the meeting. 'All right, let's get down to business. We're here to discuss our new strategy, which I'm confident will double our revenue.'

Lily starts with, 'Thank you for giving us the opportunity to present our new strategy. We've looked at it from all angles and believe it could significantly impact our revenue positively.'

HANDLING QUESTIONS

When faced with a difficult question, Jacky leans back in her chair and says, 'That's a good question. But let me explain why our approach is not just unique but incredibly effective.'

Lily leans forward when the same question comes her way. She maintains eye contact and says, 'That's an excellent question, and I'm glad you asked. It gives me an opportunity to delve deeper into our methodology.'

CLOSING THE MEETING

Jacky: 'Our strategy is unique. Let's move forward and beat the competition.'

Lily: 'We believe our strategy is strong and well-rounded, and we're open to feedback for further refinement. Together, we can achieve great results.'

POST-MEETING DEBRIEF

Jacky high-fives her teammates. 'We nailed it, didn't we?'

Lily gathers her team for a quick huddle. 'Great job, everyone. Let's keep the momentum going.'

CONCLUSION

Jacky's display of confidence is direct and assertive. She's not afraid to show ambition and uses competitive language.

Lily's confidence is shown through her preparedness, attentiveness, and ability to foster a team environment.

Neither style is better than the other; they're just different ways of displaying confidence, influenced by a variety of factors including societal expectations, upbringing, and personal preference. Both can be effective in the right context, and the best leaders often adapt their styles.

↔

There is a bigger role we play than we give ourselves credit for. While we are a minority at the workplace today, that shouldn't deter us from writing our new rules. We are proud multi-taskers, we juggle so many things successfully, and that in itself is a big source of confidence.

There is no one way to build your confidence. What you need to do is to figure out what works for you. You don't need to use the same methodology or tropes or style that men use or even what other women use.

You should select the style that feels true to you!

By incorporating these newer facets into your leadership style, you can display a multi-dimensional type of confidence that resonates with leading modern teams and challenges that are complex and ambiguous.

This is what we call rewriting the rules of confidence and feeling confident!

SUMMARY

Two types of confidence: Epistemic confidence is about how well you understand and apply knowledge, whereas social confidence is about how well you navigate and engage with the social world.

Self-Perpetuating Cycle: The sequence of events that causes women to not put themselves out there to gain confidence, and these events continue to keep the cycle in motion.
- **Initial reluctance.** Shying away from the limelight.
- **Unconscious bias.** Key decision-makers assuming that women prefer behind-the-scenes roles.
- **Missed opportunities.** Women miss out on high-visibility roles or challenging projects.
- **Lack of confidence.** Losing faith in one's abilities, making it less likely to seek the limelight in the future.
- **Perpetuation.** Patterns become ingrained, making it harder to break the cycle.

Steps to Break the Self-Perpetuating Cycle
- **Reframe the limelight.** See visibility as amplifying your impact and team achievements.
- **Challenge the unconscious bias.** Advocate for yourself and other women, disrupting outdated assumptions.
- **Be proactive.** Seek opportunities, volunteer for visibility, and don't wait to be chosen.

- **Cultivate confidence.** Build a support system, celebrate wins, and project confidence even when unsure.
- **Break the missed opportunity pattern.** Step outside your comfort zone and strategically share expertise.

REFLECT: SELF-ASSESS: ACTION

Reflect what we just discussed in the chapter above and use the following four blockers to **self-assess** where you are on the confidence journey and write out one **action** that you can take to build your self-confidence.

Sustain	Shrink
What behaviours should you continue to practice? Positive behaviours that are working well for you. For example, reading books to uplevel your expertise.	Lessen the behaviours that are not serving you well in your career. Habits that you needn't do away with but tone down. For example, starting a sentence with, 'I'm sorry, but . . .'
The behaviours I want to sustain are . . . _____ _____ _____ _____	The behaviours I want to shrink are . . . _____ _____ _____

Discard	Amplify
What is not working well for you?	What behaviours that you currently demonstrate need to be practised more?
Getting rid of behaviours that aren't working for you at all. For example, not speaking up in a team meeting or when you have a contrarian opinion.	Practices that you should do more of. For example, ensuring everyone's voice is heard in a meeting.
The behaviours I want to discard are . . .	The behaviours I want to amplify are . . .
_____	_____

Take Action

- What is your one practice that you will put into action to be more confident?

2

The Creating Visibility Rule

'My work will speak for itself.' How many of us are guilty of saying this? We would like to think that all of us at some time or the other have said or thought this. Let's look at how this was Ritu's stance for a very long time, and then things changed.

↔

Ritu's Story

In 1996, I embarked on my professional journey as a financial analyst at Gillette. As part of the role, I was set to complete two rotations within the finance function. My initial rotation in Financial Reporting was nearing its end, and I eagerly anticipated my next rotation to Treasury.

The Treasury department held an allure as it offered the opportunity to interact with senior leadership, collaborate with external bankers, and showcase my work through presentations. In essence, it promised high visibility and an opportunity to shine.

Selection for the Treasury rotation was a testament to high performance, and based on my contributions, I assumed my selection was assured. However, days before transitioning, I learned that another analyst had secured the coveted position. I was disappointed!

I approached my manager directly and expressed my disappointment in not getting the Treasury rotation. He was equally surprised, and said, 'Ritu, I wasn't aware of your desire for this role. You look so content and happy sitting in your corner, I presumed you preferred a behind-the-scenes role rather than a stakeholder-facing position. That's why I didn't consider you.'

This conversation proved to be a turning point for me. It highlighted the importance of self-advocacy and ensuring that my aspirations were known. It also underscored the value of proactive communication and dispelling any assumptions about my preferences.

More importantly, this incident, at the start of my career, left me with two valuable lessons that I have carried forward in my life:

1. Don't assume that your work alone will speak for itself. Hard work is vital, but it's equally important to be vocal about your accomplishments and aspirations.

2. You need to ask for what you want rather than hoping that people will read your mind. Don't shy away from expressing your desires and actively pursuing opportunities.

I was too young to understand the concept of being visible then, but now, I realize it was the start to my understanding the value of speaking up and voicing my thoughts, ideas, and opinions.

That's why I cringe whenever a young woman leader says, 'My work will speak for itself.' It seems nothing has changed in twenty-five years! My experience serves as a constant reminder to encourage women to be their own advocates and own their narratives.

↔

What Is Visibility and Its Importance

The Cambridge Dictionary defines visibility as 'the degree to which something is seen by the public.' In the context of the workplace, personal visibility means that people know who you are and what you can do. It also means that people know what you're good at, your skills, and knowledge. People at large have to acknowledge that something has happened, or someone has done something.

Visibility and confidence are both important and are interlinked to each other; working on one directly improves the other. However, visibility, like confidence, is a difficult topic for women leaders to navigate and work on.

Additionally, when we closely examine visibility in the corporate space, we realize that it's just not about being seen or known. Visibility takes on a new meaning. It becomes a lever for tangible gains in your career trajectory. It is not about being the loudest person in the room but about being a person who adds value to a conversation. This links the concept of visibility back to the idea of epistemic confidence that we discussed in the last chapter.

One could argue why visibility is deemed important to progress in one's career if they are the experts at their job and especially if their manager is aware of the impact their work is producing. Shouldn't meeting Key Performance Indicators (KPIs) or targets be enough?

Unfortunately, this argument doesn't win in the case of complex work settings where multiple people need to be aware of the work that you do as they have a say in your growth in the organization.

When we looked at various research on visibility and evaluated the experience of several women leaders including ourselves, we found that visibility, when done right, really helps women further their career.

In the article 'Women Don't Self-Promote, But Maybe They Should', Areen Shahbari, CEO of Shahbari Training & Consultancy and an instructor at the Harvard Extension School and Harvard DCE Professional & Executive Development, also reiterates that, 'If you don't self-promote, your contributions will probably not be visible nor recognized, which will limit your ability to get a promotion, a raise, or important projects that will help you advance in your career.'

Visibility helps with career advancement because when you and your work are known, key stakeholders and decision-makers become aware of your capabilities and contributions, and you are more likely to be in the front of their mind as a potential candidate when opportunities arise. So much so, that oftentimes, these key stakeholders become your champions who represent you and your work at forums when you may not be there.

Visibility opens doors for career advancement, salary increases, and job satisfaction and engagement. These connections are invaluable for career growth and personal development, and one that we'll talk more about in the next chapter.

Downside of Ignoring Visibility

The influence of collectivist culture shows up when there is emphasis on the objectives of the team and company rather than individual achievement. However, showcasing individual achievement is important for one's growth. Only doing good work as part of a team is not enough. It is important that your contribution is recognized and valued by the people who matter in your organization. Without enough visibility, a woman leader's achievements and capabilities might go unnoticed, affecting their career progression.

Being less visible can mean fewer opportunities to network, which can hinder both personal and professional growth. It reduces the access to meeting the right people, being invited to new opportunities, and reduced access to information and insights. Without visibility, it can be challenging to demonstrate the value one brings to the organization, which is crucial during performance evaluations or salary negotiations.

Leadership roles often require a certain level of visibility and recognition within an organization. Without it, even highly competent professionals may be overlooked for these positions. This in turn can impact self-esteem and motivation, and consequently when contributions are not acknowledged, it can lead to decreased job satisfaction and engagement.

Neglecting to invest in creating visibility for yourself can have several downsides, especially for women leaders in Asia who are already navigating a complex landscape of societal norms, workplace culture, and individual challenges. We want to acknowledge that despite advancements in gender equality and diversity initiatives, women still face numerous challenges when it comes to gaining visibility in organizations.

There are cultural norms and stereotypes on how a woman ought to show up at the workplace. These are influenced by structural barriers like lack of proper support at home leading to most women doing a 'second shift', inadequate sponsorship, and lack of role models.

A special mention must be made of the double bind that many women are caught in where they are penalized for being too visible (seen as aggressive or self-promoting) while also facing disadvantages for being less visible (missed opportunities for recognition and promotion).

Despite all of these roadblocks, in speaking to several women leaders we found that there are things within the control of women leaders that they can focus on to build visibility for themselves.

Place of Traditional Rules of Visibility in Today's World

'Blowing your own trumpet' is how visibility is traditionally defined. And most of us don't like the idea. But visibility doesn't have to be hard, doesn't have to feel inauthentic. Let's look at some ways in which visibility worked traditionally, and what practices are relevant today.

In-Person Visibility

While traditionally it was about dressing for the job, using a loud voice, or showing up at leader meetings just to be noticed, today the place of these behaviours is different. Today, speaking up in meetings to ask questions or add perspective, signing up for office hours with senior leadership to gain face time with them and to share your thoughts, or putting your hand up for high visibility projects work just as well. They help even those people who are not very vocal in large groups but prefer one-on-one interactions to speak up.

Using forums to share opinions and add value through your thoughts and expertise are as important in today's context as they were in the past. Therefore, speaking up in meetings, asking questions in meetings, and interacting with senior leadership still have a place in helping your work get noticed.

Additionally, given the advent of a hybrid workplace, how you show up on virtual meetings matters. Making sure that you have your camera on, you are appropriately dressed according to what's acceptable in your organization, making eye contact with your meeting participants, and most importantly using technology aids to make your presence known, like raising your hand to ask a question, using the chat feature to share your reactions and thoughts, etc.

Social Visibility

Traditionally, who you socialized with outside of work at events like playing golf, watching sporting events, or parties mattered because you could meet with key influential office colleagues at a personal level. Investing in thoughtful gestures and offering assistance can be strategic ways to nurture valuable relationships and enhance your visibility within your network.

While these approaches of social visibility are still in practice, today, the way social visibility is demonstrated is evolving. In the context of leadership, especially in corporate settings, social visibility continues to play a significant role. For corporate leaders, it involves being seen as an approachable, engaged, and active participant in both the internal company culture and the broader industry or public domain. This can include activities like participating in company events, being active on professional social media platforms, speaking at industry conferences, or contributing to relevant publications.

For early career to mid-career employees, participating in mentoring activities, volunteering for causes outside of work, and being part of professional networks and conferences where you meet people from your industry are important ways to increase visibility.

Cultural Visibility

Cultural visibility refers to the extent to which a person's culture is represented in society, and the ability to bring your whole self to work.

Traditionally, at the workplace the most dominant culture prevailed based on where a company was headquartered or what culture a majority of the employees came from. A person from a minority culture rarely got a chance to showcase their language, ethnicity, etc.

However, in recent times, bringing your authentic self to work has led to an openness to understanding other cultures and how they show up at work.

Building cultural visibility is no longer about showcasing your own culture but also about respecting and learning from others. While organizations now have diversity and inclusion initiatives, this is a work in progress. They attempt to ensure every employee feels free to bring their unique background to work and be themselves.

At an individual level, building cultural visibility at the workplace is a multi-faceted process that involves both personal initiative and organizational support. Given it's a newer concept, we'd like to delve deeper and share some strategies that help enhance cultural visibility:

Self-expression and advocacy

- Be open about sharing your cultural background and experiences. This could be through participating in cultural events at work, sharing stories or artefacts that represent your culture, or even through everyday conversations. Advocating for your culture and educating others about it can help increase visibility. If you're in a position to do so, advocate for policies and practices that support cultural diversity and inclusion. This can include flexible holiday policies, inclusive communication practices, or recruitment strategies that emphasize diversity.

Active participation in diversity and inclusion initiatives

- Engage with or help organize events and programmes that celebrate diversity. This could involve joining or leading a diversity and inclusion committee, organizing cultural awareness workshops, or participating in cultural celebrations at work.

Networking and building alliances

- Connect with others who share similar backgrounds or interests, and also with those from different cultures. Building a diverse network can help you gain different perspectives and increase your visibility across various cultural groups. Stay informed and educated about different cultures, including your own. This can involve attending workshops, reading, or engaging in conversations that broaden your understanding and appreciation of diversity.

Mentorship and sponsorship

- Seek mentors who can guide you in navigating the organizational culture, and in turn, mentor others. This reciprocal relationship can help in understanding different cultural dynamics and in building a more inclusive environment. If you're in a leadership role, visibly support and celebrate cultural diversity. Be a sponsor for those who may be from a minority culture and help shine light on their work. This can set a tone for the entire organization and encourage others to follow suit.

Remember, building cultural visibility is not just about showcasing your own culture, but also about respecting and learning from others. It's a continuous process that contributes significantly to personal growth and fosters a more inclusive and dynamic organizational environment.

REWRITE THE RULES

We know that even with the evolution of the traditional rules of visibility, it can be hard for women leaders to find ways that feel authentic and natural to them. Many women leaders we spoke to have mastered the art of visibility on their terms, therefore, rewriting the rules of visibility to work for them, and we'll share those rewritten rules with you here.

Voice Your Opinion

Whether it's in team meetings, one-on-one conversations, webinars, or conferences, by voicing your opinions and offering insights you can create a strong presence. Make your points clearly, but also remember that being open to other perspectives is important.

Sometimes opportunities are not given but have to be taken. So, if you see a high-visibility project, express your interest and raise your hand.

Use these forums to also broaden and diversify your network to include influential people who can vouch for your skills and contributions. We will talk about networks in our next chapter.

↔

Rajita's Story

The transition to my new role and team presented initial challenges. Adjusting to unfamiliar responsibilities and dynamics was daunting, and I initially found myself hesitant to contribute actively. The fear of my ideas not being fully developed or resonant with the team led me to adopt a more passive approach in larger meetings. I focused primarily on absorbing information and observing the team's established communication patterns, hoping to gain a stronger understanding before actively participating.

During a one-on-one session, my manager's insightful question pierced through my carefully constructed facade. 'Rajita,' she said, her voice laced with gentle concern, 'I see you brimming with ideas during our meetings, yet I rarely hear your voice in the larger discussions. Why is that?'

Initially, I attempted to justify my silence by citing my preference for observation and information gathering. However, my manager saw through my veiled explanation. 'Rajita,' she stated with empathy, 'if you don't actively share your insights, your value may remain unrecognized. Imagine the positive impact you could have on the organization by leveraging your unique perspective.'

Her words shifted the focus from my own anxieties to the potential I held to contribute. It wasn't about proving myself, but about offering my insights for the betterment of the team. This realization ignited a spark within me—a determination to overcome my self-doubt and amplify my voice.

Stepping outside my comfort zone felt like scaling a mountain. I started by setting a small, achievable goal:

speak up and share my point of view at least five times during every meeting. Using tally marks on a notepad, I tracked my progress, with each mark serving as a testament to my growing confidence.

With each spoken word, the fear that had previously held me back began to diminish. My voice, once hesitant and barely audible, gained strength and clarity. As my contributions were recognized and valued, I was invited to participate in key projects—opportunities that significantly advanced my career.

The journey from self-doubt to self-assuredness wasn't an overnight transformation, but a gradual evolution fuelled by courage and a belief in my own potential. It taught me that the most impactful voices are often the ones that choose to speak up, to share their unique perspectives, and to contribute to the collective good.

↔

Find a Sponsor

Unlike mentors who guide you, sponsors advocate for you. A sponsor can be instrumental in getting you high-visibility projects and promotions. McKinsey's article 'Closing the gap: Leadership perspectives on promoting women in financial services' shows that sponsorship is a key factor in advancing women's careers:

The 2017 Women in the Workplace research showed that women who receive advice from managers and senior leaders on career advancement are more likely to be promoted, and yet earlier-tenure women receive less encouragement and support from managers and senior leaders in advancing their careers than do their male peers. Such encouragement and support can make all the difference.

Therefore, instead of waiting for sponsorship to happen to you, you need to take the initiative to find a sponsor who can advocate for you in places that matter. Therefore, the role of networking and mentorship can't be overstated in the pursuit of finding the right sponsor for yourself.

If you are already in a middle or top-level management position, don't forget to pay forward by mentoring other women. Not only do you become a role model, but this also helps build a network of people who can speak for you.

↔

Here is what we heard from Ami Moris on how sponsorship helped her move forward in her career. Ami is based in Malaysia and has recently retired from the role of the chief executive officer of Maybank Investment Banking Group. Currently she serves on the board of several companies in Malaysia.

> Being born in the year of the ox instilled a strong work ethic in me. However, early in my career, expressing my opinions directly often felt like a tightrope walk. Suppressing my fiery spirit and learning to communicate assertively were constant challenges. Looking back, I know I stumbled many times, but these experiences were stepping stones on the path to effective leadership.
>
> Through reflection, I learned the importance of bringing diverse perspectives together. This realization, however, led me to a crucial insight for Asian women leaders: The need to invest in social capital.
>
> Building social capital goes beyond simply making connections. It's about women strategically investing in themselves and their visibility. This requires confidence, a curated network of influential people, and a well-defined personal brand.
>
> For many Asian women, these activities can feel unnatural. We often prioritize family time, and traditional networking events—like karaoke nights with clients—

may not resonate with us. Moreover, voicing dissent can carry a double burden—reinforcing stereotypes about Asian women's assertiveness.

Navigating this complex landscape requires clarity on your personal brand. What do you stand for? What value do you bring? Identifying these elements allows you to strategically target individuals whose opinions and influence matter to your career goals. These are your potential sponsors.

Having a sponsor, male or female, is a game-changer. Sponsors are champions who vouch for your abilities, values, and potential. They advocate for you in boardrooms, ensuring your contributions are recognized and propelling you to the next level.

For young Asian women considering leadership roles, investing in social capital might seem like a chore. But trust me, it's not. Hard work alone won't guarantee promotions in boardrooms. Visibility and advocacy are essential. Those who consistently put themselves in front of decision-makers are the ones who come to mind when opportunities arise.

↔

Be Proactive

The benefits of visibility often manifest over time, which can make it difficult for busy leaders to prioritize this aspect of their career development. They might be so engrossed in day-to-day operations or immediate responsibilities that they overlook the long-term advantages.

Therefore, the trick is to first frame creating visibility not as a 'nice-to-have' but as a strategic 'must-have'. This way you don't miss any opportunity to showcase your work.

Also remember you can be visible while being authentic. There are several gender stereotypes related to women advocating for themselves and being visible. Some common examples are:

- When a woman confidently advocates for herself or her ideas, she might be seen as 'aggressive' or 'bossy', while a man exhibiting the same behaviour might be considered 'assertive' or 'strong'.
- Or women may be seen as 'oversharing' or 'boasting' their accomplishments if they talk about them too much, but if they downplay their achievements, they might be perceived as lacking ambition.

By not doing what you should to be visible perpetuates the stereotypes further. To challenge these preconceived notions, proactively showcase your competence and leadership abilities. Many Asian women leaders have international experiences, which allows them to uniquely blend Western and Eastern leadership styles effectively.

↔

Zalina Jamaluddin is the vice president at Hibiscus Petroleum Berhad, Malaysia. Zalina has extensive experience and has worked in different industries in Malaysia. The anecdote she shared with us highlights the power of a proactive approach to visibility.

Early in my career, a supervisor at ExxonMobil gave me a piece of advice that stuck: 'Zalina, you need to be more visible.' At twenty-three, fresh out of college, I wasn't sure what that meant. Visibility? Personal brand? These weren't concepts we discussed back in 2000.

Being a A-type personality, I took this advice seriously. But the traditional networking route—the pushy, self-promotional approach—didn't resonate with me. I wanted to create visibility on my own terms.

The answer? Demonstrating my value. It wasn't about bragging; it was about showcasing my skills and becoming a resource for others. This genuine approach felt more natural and rewarding than aggressive self-promotion.

Instead of the traditional networking route of attending industry events, I took a more proactive approach. I volunteered for challenging assignments, exceeding expectations and showcasing my abilities. I also actively offered my expertise and assistance to colleagues, establishing myself as a helpful and reliable resource.

Through this proactive approach, I discovered my natural strengths: connection and mentorship. My diverse industry experience allowed me to connect people across silos, becoming a valuable bridge within the company. Additionally, my passion for personal development led colleagues to seek me out for advice and guidance. I focused on these two strengths, offering genuine service and value to others.

This proactive approach to visibility paid off. My reputation for being a connector and a mentor spread organically through word-of-mouth and informal networks. Instead of the traditional resume and application route, 100 per cent of my career opportunities came from my established network and the value I consistently delivered.

My career path hasn't been a straight line. I've transitioned between industries, embracing a zigzagging approach. But building visibility through value has allowed me to navigate these changes and forge a successful career path on my own terms.

↔

A lot of the Asian women leaders we spoke to leverage the unique advantage that they have from working in non-Asian countries. For instance, these Asian women leaders are leveraging the direct and open communication style, while fostering relationship-building and harmony within the team. Similarly, they are implementing a consultative process while still retaining the final say.

By drawing on both Western and Eastern approaches, Asian women leaders can create a leadership style that is effective, adaptable, and inclusive. The key is to find a balance that leverages the strengths of both Eastern and Western leadership styles.

By now, we hope you appreciate the value of building visibility both within and outside your organization and agree that it is a powerful tool for driving personal and professional growth. Doing so allows you to share your expertise, connect with valuable networks, and explore new opportunities that can propel your career forward. By proactively seeking out opportunities to be seen and heard, you open yourself to exciting possibilities for growth and career advancement.

Now we'd like to share a matrix of specific tools and ways to build visibility in the new age of leadership.

Leadership Visibility Matrix

This is a framework (see *Figure 2*) that combines three key elements to elevate your presence and propel your career. Let's look at each element in detail.

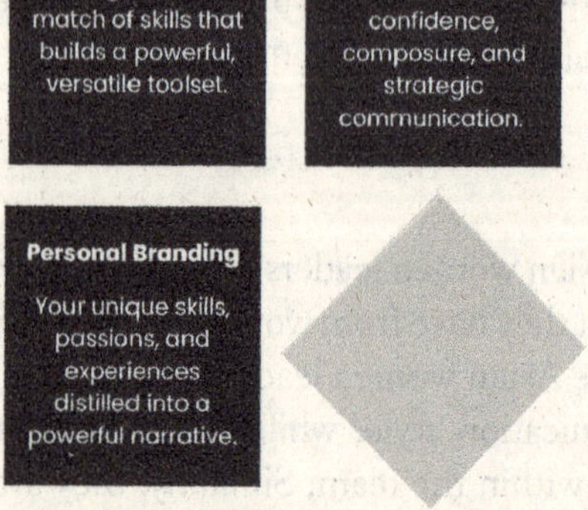

Leadership Visibility Matrix

Skills Stacking
A strategic mix-and-match of skills that builds a powerful, versatile toolset.

Executive Presence
A nuanced blend of confidence, composure, and strategic communication.

Personal Branding
Your unique skills, passions, and experiences distilled into a powerful narrative.

Figure 2

Skill Stacking

When you are applying for a new role or job, your resume is your first point of visibility, and chances are that when writing your resume, you followed a standard template and listed your skills in a generic manner. But what if we told you that instead of looking at your skills as discrete entities, you should look at them holistically, combining them to create a unique set that will make you stand out. An unexpected combination of skills can pique an employer's interest and prompt them to read your resume more closely. This can open the door for an interview where you can elaborate on how the combination of your skills can benefit the company.

Scott Adams, the creator of the famous Dilbert comic strip, introduced a concept he calls 'Talent Stacking' or 'Skill Stacking'. Instead of aiming to be the best in the world at one particular skill, which can be incredibly challenging, Adams suggests that individuals can become uniquely valuable by acquiring a combination of 'good-enough' skills that work well together.

Imagine someone who is:

- A good public speaker (but not the best)
- Proficient at writing (but not a bestselling author)
- Understands the basics of marketing (but isn't a guru)

Individually, these skills might not make someone stand out. But the combination can make this person a highly sought-after corporate trainer, keynote speaker, or facilitator.

Another example could be of a leader who is technically savvy, not a subject matter expert but is still able to communicate effectively. Being able to communicate complex technical concepts in a way that is understandable to non-technical stakeholders is a rare skill.

When we work with women leaders through our programme, we use skill stacking as a tool to help them build their unique brand and hence create visibility.

In rapidly changing corporate landscapes, having a diverse skill set allows women leaders to pivot easily, contributing in various capacities and thus maintaining high visibility. The key is to be visible not just in one area that you're the best in but in several complementary areas.

↔

For instance, when we spoke to Pei Lin Cho, managing director, APRW—a PR agency in Singapore—about her career journey, we saw that it illustrated the concept of deliberately expanding into new complementary skill areas as she took on new challenges and opportunities over the course of her career. Her ability to skill-stack enabled greater impact.

> Pei Lin is based in Singapore, and as a communication strategist she has extensive experience in crisis, disputes & litigation matters, government relations, causes & non-profit work.
>
> Pei Lin leveraged her background as a lawyer when she transitioned into the public relations industry. Her critical thinking, presentation, and advocacy skills from law translated well even though she was learning an entirely new field.
>
> When Pei Lin became an entrepreneur starting her PR agency, she suddenly had to pick up skills like HR, finance, operations, rather than just focusing on PR-related skills. This demonstrated how she was stacking complementary business skills on top of her existing expertise. As Pei Lin took on more senior leadership roles managing teams, new skills like 'servant leadership', executive communication abilities, and strategy development stacked on top of her previous experience.

Over time, Pei Lin added substantial non-profit/ community service work and board governance skills to her existing corporate talents to create a fuller portfolio.

↔

There are many such examples of leaders combining their subject matter expertise with either communication skills, content creation skills, marketing skills, etc., and creating a set of skills that make them unique.

For women leaders aiming to increase their visibility, this approach is especially powerful. It's about creating a unique blend of skills that enables them to stand out and be recognized for their diverse contributions. Skill stacking encourages them to leverage all their talents, not just those directly related to their job descriptions.

Let's see how different skills that we build over the years can be put to use at the workplace.

Skill Transfer

Prior to becoming part of the workplace, we are all exposed to different forms of art, sports, and leisure activities, and are encouraged to pick something up to develop outside of the school curriculum. The environment at home too sometimes encourages children to participate in activities like cooking, gardening, repairs, etc.

Later in life it is the skills that you pick up from these activities that we bring to our work lives as well, and this is what we mean by skill transfer.

For instance, you learn resilience and the value of hard work from repeatedly failing, practising, and overcoming obstacles when you pick up a sport or musical instrument. You learn teamwork, collaboration, delegation, conflict resolution when you play a team sport or work on projects together. Activities like art and music help hone your creative side that helps with creative thinking at work. Through these activities you meet with diverse groups of people, and you can build your network and establish valuable connections. These relationships can be beneficial for finding career opportunities and gaining insights into your chosen field.

The key to successful skill transfer is reflection and identification. By critically analysing the skills you develop through various activities, you can understand how they are relevant to your career aspirations and actively leverage them in your job search and professional development.

↔

Rajita's Story

My life has been a journey of multifaceted learning. While formal education in medicine served as the foundation, the diverse skill set that I cultivated throughout my life has complemented my education.

Early immersion in the structured world of Indian classical music instilled in me the invaluable qualities of discipline, focus, and creativity. Beyond the realm of music, my other artistic pursuits like painting and writing also served as fertile ground for nurturing my creative and communication skills, as well as for fostering lateral thinking and problem-solving abilities.

Yoga became a transformative practice that did not just enhance physical well-being but also honed resilience and adaptability. These qualities became my compass, guiding me through professional challenges and enabling me to navigate the stress and complexities of the corporate world.

As I worked with teams, I explored the realm of coaching to further refine my ability to analyse, understand, and motivate individuals to reach their full potential. These skills proved invaluable in my leadership roles, allowing me to build high-performing teams, and foster a culture of growth and inclusivity within my organization.

Looking back, I recognize the transformative power of diverse experiences. From formal education to artistic pursuits and personal growth endeavours, each activity has contributed to a robust skill set that defines who I am today. This ever-evolving skill set provides me with the strength, adaptability, and resilience to navigate the ever-changing landscape of life.

These experiences also helped me build my network, which has been a constant source of support and inspiration, offering invaluable insights and unexpected solutions throughout my career and providing me with the visibility for growth opportunities.

I believe that my story serves as a testament to the power of lifelong learning and skill transfer.

↔

To summarize, we believe that extracurricular activities and activities at home, while seemingly unrelated to your career goals, can play a crucial role in developing valuable skills, exploring interests, and shaping you into a well-rounded individual. And remember, it's never too late to pick up a new hobby or to start off what you left behind a while ago.

These experiences can be showcased on your resume and during job interviews, setting you apart from other candidates and giving you a competitive edge in the job market.

Executive Presence

Executive presence is often considered one of the 'intangibles' of leadership, but its impact on visibility is far-reaching.

Essentially, executive presence is about how a leader carries themselves, communicates, and engages with others. It encompasses attributes such as confidence, poise, decisiveness, and emotional intelligence.

Executive presence is crucial for building visibility because a strong executive presence often leaves a lasting impression, helping leaders gain attention, respect, and influence among team members, stakeholders, and even competitors. When you walk into a room with gravitas, people are more likely to pay attention to what you have to say, increasing your visibility and impact.

People are more likely to follow leaders who exhibit qualities like confidence, authenticity, and empathy—the core components of executive presence. This trust and credibility are vital for building a leadership brand that's not just visible but also effective.

In a sea of managers and leaders, a compelling executive presence helps you stand out. It distinguishes you as not just a manager who oversees tasks but as a leader who inspires action and followership. This is especially vital in large organizations where visibility can be a challenge because you are one of many managers.

As the McKinsey Global Institute report titled 'The power of parity: Advancing women's equality in Asia Pacific' states, there is only one woman for every four men in leadership positions in Asia. Since women are underrepresented in senior leadership roles across various sectors, a compelling executive presence can serve as a differentiator. When you're competing for senior positions, a strong executive presence can make you more visible to decision-makers within the organization.

With a strong executive presence, your opinions carry more weight, your suggestions are taken more seriously, and you become more persuasive. This is essential when you are negotiating, doing strategic planning, and leading change initiatives.

As more women ascend to leadership roles, they serve as role models for others. A strong executive presence not only helps individual women but can also pave the way for other aspiring women leaders.

In professional settings we see that social expectations often portray men as inherently more confident, an attribute frequently associated with executive presence. However, this perception overlooks the crucial distinction between confidence and competence. While men may be encouraged to project confidence, women, despite being equally competent, may often downplay their achievements, potentially impacting the perception of their executive presence.

This discrepancy stems from ingrained societal biases that associate confidence and assertiveness with masculinity, while attributing humility and self-deprecation to femininity. This conditioning can lead women to understate their accomplishments and hesitate to claim their rightful space in leadership roles.

However, true executive presence goes beyond outward displays of confidence. It is a multifaceted quality encompassing competence, strategic thinking, decisiveness, and the ability to inspire and motivate others. Women can cultivate these essential skills and project executive presence by:

Owning their accomplishments

- Women should confidently acknowledge their achievements and contributions, instead of downplaying their successes. Articulating their expertise and value proposition effectively demonstrates their competence and leadership potential.

Embracing their unique strengths

- Women often possess a diverse range of strengths, such as strong interpersonal skills, emotional intelligence, and collaborative leadership styles. Recognizing and leveraging these strengths can create a distinct and impactful leadership presence.

Communicating with clarity and conviction

- Women should communicate their ideas and opinions with clarity and conviction, avoiding self-deprecating language or apologizing for their contributions. This fosters an aura of authority and inspires confidence in both themselves and others.

Building a strong network

- Connecting with mentors, sponsors, and other influential individuals can provide valuable guidance, support, and opportunities for women to showcase their expertise and develop their leadership skills.

By recognizing the difference between confidence and competence, and embracing their unique strengths, women can redefine executive presence in their own terms. By owning their accomplishments, communicating with conviction, and building strong networks, they can shatter outdated stereotypes and pave the way for a more inclusive and equitable leadership landscape.

And as the conversation around leadership becomes more inclusive, the attributes traditionally associated with women, such as collaboration, empathy, and emotional intelligence, are increasingly being recognized as valuable components of executive presence.

Remember that executive presence is about leaving a mark by intentionally showing up, bringing together your brand and your communication and leadership styles. It's not just about climbing the corporate ladder but about shifting perceptions, influencing outcomes, and driving change in a meaningful way.

In short, it's a key tool in your leadership toolkit for visibility.

↔

Here's what we heard from Fanny Huang—VP Strategic Deals & Head of ESG APAC, DHL Supply Chain at DHL—on executive presence. Prior to DHL, Fanny has worked both in Europe and Singapore based organizations.

Her story demonstrates that 'softer skills' are more than just career tools; they're valuable life skills. By investing in them early on, you develop an executive presence that propels you forward and allows you to make a lasting impact.

Looking back, I can see how much kinder I could have been to myself early on in my career. While I wasn't naturally shy, being an Asian woman in a predominantly international consulting environment presented a unique challenge: finding my voice.

One significant challenge arose when I transitioned from an Asian to a European work environment. The 'softer skills' I honed back when I started working, like communication and active listening, proved invaluable. However, while never truly quiet, I initially struggled to find my voice amidst the assertive communication style prevalent in European management consulting. The pressure to contribute and demonstrate expertise was immense. This realization forced me out of my comfort zone.

I learned to navigate this dynamic by strategically finding opportunities to speak up, leveraging my self-awareness of my own strengths. The key was not to always present groundbreaking ideas, but instead to frame existing viewpoints and guide discussions effectively.

Active listening became my secret weapon, allowing me to gather insight and then interject with well-considered perspectives. Beyond technical skills, soft skills like communication, framing ideas, and active listening have been instrumental throughout my career.

These skills, coupled with strong presentation skills, are the foundation of executive presence. Honing

these abilities early on equipped me to engage with
senior stakeholders and solidify my presence in the
professional arena.

↔

Personal Brand

What's a personal brand? It is famously said that, 'What people
say about you when you are not in the room is your brand.' All
of us already have a brand that we may or may not be aware of,
therefore, if we are not intentional then that perception about
us becomes our brand.

In Ritu's story shared at the start of this chapter, her
manager perceived Ritu to be the 'quiet one' who likes to sit
behind her desk and work. She hadn't built that brand but that's
the perception that was created. This illustrates why building
a personal brand is so important for creating visibility. If you
don't do it yourself, then it is done for you.

Personal branding often opens doors to new opportunities,
such as high impact projects, partnerships, or career
advancements. At the same time, lack of branding can result
in these chances going to others who are more visible. Building
a personal brand doesn't have to feel inauthentic; it's about
amplifying who you already are and aligning your actions with
your values and expertise.

Here are some tips on how to intentionally build your brand
to create the right visibility.

Start with self-reflection

- Identify your unique skills, values, and passions. Align
  your brand with what genuinely matters to you—
  this will ensure that it feels authentic. Focus on what
  you're good at and how those skills meet a need in the
  marketplace. Playing to your strengths ensures that
  your brand is rooted in genuine competency.

Craft your narrative

- Develop a compelling story that communicates your journey, values, and aspirations. We experienced the power of stories when we recorded our podcast, all the leaders on it had such powerful and insightful stories to share. Stories are a powerful tool and all of us have stories! Ensure that your messaging is consistent across different platforms and interactions. Consistency builds trust, and trust is the cornerstone of any strong brand.

Add value to others

- Share insights, offer help, and build relationships without expecting immediate returns. You can build social capital and demonstrate leadership without coming across as self-serving. Actively engage with peers, mentors, and influencers in your industry. This not only expands your network but also provides you with different perspectives that can help you refine your brand.

Seek feedback

- Regularly ask for feedback to understand how you're perceived. Feedback provides valuable insights into potential areas for refinement. This is an important step in making sure your brand is perceived the way you want it to be.

We would recommend that you see personal branding as another form of leadership skill development, at par with decision-making, team management, or strategic planning.

Leveraging Digital Platforms for Maximum Visibility

In today's digitally connected world, it would be remiss to not talk about using digital platforms to create visibility. Learning how to leverage social media and professional networks to share insights, stories, or articles related to your culture or cultural diversity in general can help in reaching a wider audience.

There are many new avenues for gaining visibility thanks to technological advancements and changes in the way we work. Here are some ways to increase your visibility digitally:

Professional social networking sites

- Ensure you have an updated profile on Professional Social Networking platforms like LinkedIn, Indeed, Glassdoor, etc. Utilize the platform to write articles/posts on topics you are passionate about or relevant to your industry thus reaching a broad, professional audience.

Personal websites or blogs

- Create a digital portfolio or thought leadership platform to showcase achievements, ideas, and expertise.

Participate in panels, webinars, conferences

- Say yes to the invitations to speak in panels and conferences. With virtual panels and webinars, you can participate without geographical constraints and reach a wider audience.

Podcasting

- Host or appear on podcasts relevant to your field. It can enhance your credibility and reach.

Collaborative projects

- Work on co-authored reports, studies, or write papers to share your expertise and increase visibility.

The new age of visibility is multi-dimensional, it blends traditional avenues with digital platforms and community engagement. These new methods not only offer increased opportunities for visibility but also enable more targeted and meaningful interactions. Digital visibility also works for leaders who are shy or are introverts and don't enjoy the limelight.

Gone are the days when success for women leaders in Asia solely relied on conforming to traditional norms of visibility. Today, these remarkable individuals are skilfully shifting paradigms and crafting a hybrid model of leadership that thrives on both effectiveness and deep cultural understanding.

↔

We'd like to highlight the story of Professor Sun Sun Lim, vice president of Partnerships & Engagement at Singapore Management University (SMU), where she is concurrently the professor of Communication and Technology at College of Integrative Studies. Based in Singapore, she was recently conferred the inaugural Asia Top 50 Women Tech Leaders Award 2024 and named Fellow of Singapore Computer Society.

She shared that maintaining visibility throughout her career has been a continuous journey of adaptation and learning. By embracing new technologies, prioritizing self-care, and leveraging supportive networks, she's been able to navigate the challenges and carve out a successful path in academia.

Early in my academic career, the pressure was immense. As an assistant professor vying for tenure, I needed to establish myself as a valuable contributor—a scholar with impactful research, strong student mentorship skills, and the potential to lead the academic community in the future.

This 'tenure push' coincided with a particularly demanding time in my personal life—the arrival of my two children. While I was fortunate to have a supportive academic husband who took on more childcare responsibilities as I neared tenure, the challenge of maintaining visibility remained.

In academia, research can have global implications. Building a strong reputation requires actively participating in international conferences and interacting with international peers. However, with young children at home, travelling for long conferences across continents seemed like an impossible feat.

Thankfully, social media emerged during this critical period. It offered a new platform for interaction with colleagues between conferences. However, this presented a new kind of visibility challenge: the need to cultivate and maintain an active online public profile.

Balancing research, publishing, promoting my work online, and the demands of family life was a constant struggle. I learned the importance of prioritizing self-care. Now, I schedule regular exercise sessions in my calendar, treating them as essential appointments, not just optional activities. This not only keeps me physically healthy but also provides crucial thinking time away from screens.

Managing an online presence requires finding your comfort zone. While Facebook proved valuable for both professional and personal connections within my academic community, Twitter's (now X) fast-paced anonymity caused me undue stress. I learned to choose platforms that aligned with my communication style and goals.

↔

No One Way

Based on our research we have come to the conclusion that there is 'no one way' to build visibility. You have to find what works best for you. The path to visibility is often a blend of individual personality, cultural factors, organizational dynamics, and even societal norms. What works wonderfully for one person could backfire for another.

↔

To illustrate this, let's look at two fictional women leaders—Emily and Priya—both talented, both ambitious, and both new hires at GlobalTech Corp. They have different approaches to creating visibility at work.

Emily's Journey

Stepping into the bustling office, Emily carried a mix of cautious optimism. New to the company, she navigated the sea of faces, eager to find her place. The welcome luncheon for new hires offered a chance to connect. While others gravitated towards the C-suite, Emily sought out her immediate team.

Focusing on team building, she actively listened, learning about their roles, challenges, and even their favourite hobbies. This deliberate approach built rapport and created a foundation for future collaboration.

Instead of jumping into the spotlight, Emily patiently observed the company's rhythm. After a month, she carefully chose her first project, one she knew she could excel at. This calculated risk allowed her to showcase her skills without overstepping.

In meetings, Emily strategically asserted herself, using phrases like 'Based on my experience, I feel we should . . .' This balanced approach ensured her voice was heard while maintaining a collaborative tone.

Beyond her immediate duties, Emily recognized a gap. She launched a blog series highlighting the 'Unsung Heroes' in the tech industry, focusing on diversity and inclusion. This initiative resonated with colleagues and gained external traction, showcasing her vision and leadership potential.

Guided by intuition, Emily found a mentor in Karen, a seasoned manager. Karen became her advocate, championing her accomplishments in leadership meetings. This invaluable sponsorship helped Emily navigate the company's power dynamics and accelerated her progress.

Emily's journey, though deliberate, was marked by steady progress. She transitioned from a cautious beginner to a rising star, proving that strategic action, coupled with humility and collaborative spirit, paves the path to success.

Priya's Journey

Priya strode into GlobalTech Corp brimming with confidence. The welcome luncheon was no mere formality; it was a chance to make her mark. With a captivating smile and a firm handshake, she introduced herself to department heads, even venturing to engage the CEO in conversation.

Within a week, Priya's ambition manifested. She didn't just volunteer for a high-risk project, she spearheaded it. Her confidence, fuelled by past successes, radiated outwards, inspiring her team and captivating her superiors.

Meetings became Priya's platform. She spoke confidently, weaving past experiences and accomplishments into the discussion, establishing her credibility and expertise. This assertive approach, though unconventional, commanded attention and earned respect.

Beyond the company walls, Priya's ambition extended to the digital realm. Her LinkedIn profile became a dynamic showcase of her work. She shared every project, wrote insightful posts on industry trends, and celebrated her achievements with pride, subtly but effectively branding herself as an industry expert.

Priya's proactive approach attracted not just colleagues, but also champions. Tom, a senior executive, recognized her potential and became her unwavering advocate. He sang her praises in leadership meetings, ensuring her voice was heard and her contributions recognized.

Priya's journey wasn't just about talent, it was about strategy. Her confidence, coupled with calculated actions and a keen eye for connections, propelled her through the ranks of GlobalTech Corp. She was not just climbing the ladder; she was building her own staircase to success.

By the end of the first year, both Emily and Priya have increased their visibility, but in very different ways. Emily's approach was community-oriented, cautious, and nuanced, while Priya was assertive, direct, and open to take risks.

Emily gains visibility as a thoughtful leader who brings value to her team and the broader community. Priya gains visibility as a go-getter, someone who is unafraid to take risks and put herself out there.

And so, their stories unfold, each finding their own way to stand out, to lead, and to make a difference in their unique styles.

Emily and Priya illustrate that different approaches can still lead to the same outcome—greater visibility and career advancement. The key is to tailor your strategy to your strengths, your work environment, and your personal comfort level with risk. We found this in our conversation with women leaders too; everyone had their unique style of building visibility.

SUMMARY

Importance of visibility: Visibility unlocks career advancement. When people know you and your work, you're top of mind for opportunities. Key stakeholders become your champions, advocating for you even when you're not in the room.

The Leadership Visibility Matrix: A powerful combination

- **Skill stacking.** Strategically combining your skills and experiences to create a versatile toolbox, unlocking new possibilities and demonstrating your adaptability.
- **Executive presence.** The quiet confidence, composure, and strategic communication that commands respect and trust, making you a natural leader.
- **Personal branding.** Crafting a compelling narrative that showcases your unique skills, passions, and value, attracting opportunities and building your network.

Digital visibility: In today's connected world, your digital footprint matters. Building your online presence like a professional portfolio, showcasing your accomplishments, sharing insights, and engaging with your network. It's about owning your narrative and proactively shaping your online reputation.

REFLECT: SELF-ASSESS: ACTION

Reflect what we just discussed in the chapter above and use the following four blockers to **self-assess** where you are on the visibility journey and write out one **action** that you can take to build your visibility.

Sustain	Shrink
What behaviours should you continue to practice? Positive behaviours that are working well for you. For example, regularly posting thought leadership articles on LinkedIn. The behaviours I want to sustain are . . . _____ _____ _____	What behaviours are not serving you well? Habits that you want to see less of. For example, keeping your camera switched off during meetings. The behaviours I want to shrink are . . . _____ _____ _____
Discard	**Amplify**
What is not working well for you? Getting rid of behaviours that aren't working for you at all. For example, not seeking feedback from mentors to improve. The behaviours I want to discard are . . . _____ _____ _____	What behaviours that you currently demonstrate need to be practised more? Practices that you should do more of. For example, showcase your complementary skills. The behaviours I want to amplify are . . . _____ _____ _____

Take Action

- What is your one practice that you will put into action to create visibility?

3

The Building Network Rule

My experience of building networks in China differed significantly from my experience at Shiseido. In China, I had already spent ten years within the same organization. I had a well-established network of colleagues in the regional office, built on years of mutual trust and respect. My primary challenge there was leading the local team and fostering trust within that specific group. Additionally, I needed to maintain the strong relationships with Chinese retailers, crucial for our business success.

However, at Shiseido, it was a whole new ball game. It was a leap outside my comfort zone. My experience was deeply seated in beauty business and within the travel retail channel. Hence, entering a new company and a new channel of business were the unknowns. This meant that I had to re-establish my network within the company and with new business partners. Within the organization, understanding how internal networks, both formal and informal, function was really key. Hence, it was also about knowing and understanding which members of the team can help you within those networks.

Let's be honest, I'm an introvert. Building networks doesn't come naturally to me. But I believe this is a common challenge for many women. Within a long-established organization, the network already exists. The real difficulty lies in building external networks with industry partners and colleagues in a new company. This requires pushing yourself out of your comfort zone.

Now, within a corporate role, building internal networks is also critical. You need to be visible, understand the impact you can make, and be willing to build relationships. This internal network proved especially crucial when I joined Shiseido without existing connections.

While many of us would want to drive change and transformation quickly when we take on a new role, it is equally critical to understand and leverage what existing teams and resources can bring. Tapping on and learning to leverage the existing network of experienced teams really helped me to navigate the organization more smoothly. Hence, my belief is that it's important to understand the value of resources and the power of internal networks.

This account was shared with us by Nicole Tan, who is the president & CEO at Shiseido APAC, and notably the first woman regional CEO at Shiseido. She is based in Singapore and comes with over twenty-five years of beauty industry experience. Nicole's story showcases how building connections helps with career growth.

↔

Why Networking?

When it comes to networking in relation to work, it's seen that women are reluctant to do so just for the sake of networking. You rarely hear of the 'girls club' or some such gathering akin to the 'old boys club'. This is despite women generally being more wired to relate to others through higher emotional intelligence, empathy, vulnerability—all aspects that are required to form deeper connections.

Networking when simply viewed as making new connections for the sake of it or getting people to do you favours isn't something that appeals to everyone.

So, right at the start we'd like to reframe that thought and instead think of networking as building connections and meaningful relationships at work, rather than something that is transactional or mercenary in nature.

The psychology of connection is a fundamental aspect of human behaviour and has implications on various aspects of life including personal development, social interactions, and mental health. At its core, it is the need to belong. This basic human drive is as essential as the need for food and shelter. Forming connections with others fulfils this need and contributes to a sense of identity and community.

Medical research too has shown that fostering connections is critical to health and wellness. Strong social connections are linked to positive mental health outcomes. They provide emotional support, reduce stress, and contribute to a sense of belonging. In fact, the impact of an isolated, lonely life on our health is worse than that of smoking, high blood pressure, or obesity. The need to connect is a human need, and every person needs connections in their lives in the workplace and at home.

In this chapter, let's explore how women leaders have navigated the paradigm of building networks and used their innate ability to form deep connections to build their network, or maybe even changed the definition of networking!

↔

Ritu's Story

I moved to Singapore in 2014 with two things: my family and a big dream of starting my own coaching business. Quitting my corporate job felt amazing, but it also meant starting completely over. New country, new industry, and no professional network to speak of. Even my LinkedIn profile was pretty sad—only 300 connections!

But I knew the saying, 'A journey of a thousand miles begins with a single step.' Singapore has a robust learning culture and communities, so, my first step was to join a local coaching group. We met once a month, and it was a great way to meet new people. These initial connections led to introductions to other people. My network slowly grew bigger, and the connections just kept getting stronger.

The best part? It all felt natural. We had real conversations, shared our stories, and built friendships, not just business connections. As my network grew on LinkedIn too, I knew I was on the right track.

I didn't just stick to the coaching group, though. I joined online forums, went to events, and even met people for coffee chats—the old-fashioned way! My approach was simple: listen, learn, and find things we had in common. It wasn't just about building business connections; it was about building friendships.

And guess what? The power of connections really surprised me. Before I knew it, I had built a strong network.

Even when we started writing this book and our podcast, we didn't have a lot to go on. We only had interviews with a few women leaders we knew personally. But we weren't afraid to ask for referrals. Every connection led to another, and pretty soon, our network exploded. We ended up interviewing over 200 amazing women in the region, and their stories are full of inspiration and wisdom. That's the magic of building relationships—they open doors you never knew existed.

Looking back, that seemingly daunting task became a rewarding journey. Sure, I'm no networking expert, but my experience unearthed three key lessons:

Let relationships grow naturally

- While strategies are helpful, genuine connections flourish under the warmth of authenticity.

One-on-one interactions have superpowers

- Deep conversations in individual settings forge stronger bonds than any large-scale event.

Consistency is key

- Building a network is a marathon, not a sprint. Show up, engage, and nurture those connections—it's a gradual dance, not a frantic hustle.

So, there you have it: my story of building a network from scratch, brick by genuine brick. Take your first step, embrace the one-on-one, be authentic, and watch your network grow, organic and meaningful, just like mine.

↔

The Benefits of Networking

In the context of work, networking is about building and nurturing professional relationships that are mutually beneficial, because a strong network is not just about what you can get but what you can give as well. When you interact with various people in your field for information exchange, advice, and support, both you as the initiator and the person you reached out to benefit

There are many benefits of networking in a professional setting that are influenced by the collectivist culture seen in Asia that promotes a strong emphasis on social cohesion and support networks.

Career development and business opportunities

- Networking can help you advance your careers by providing insights into job opportunities, offering guidance for professional growth, and facilitating mentoring relationships. Whether you are an entrepreneur or a business professional, networking can be a key tool for finding new clients, partners, or investors that can lead to business collaborations.

Knowledge exchange and resource accessibility

- By networking you can exchange industry-specific knowledge, insights, and best practices, and this continuous learning helps you stay informed about the latest trends and developments in your field. You may gain access to resources that you weren't aware of or that might not be available otherwise. This access to information, expertise, manpower, or even financial resources opens up more opportunities for you.

Building a professional identity and thought leadership

- Networking contributes to the development of a personal brand. If you recollect, in the chapter on visibility, we spoke about how your personal brand can open the doors of career opportunities for you.
- Networking with others allows you to showcase your skills, expertise, and values to a broader audience, enhancing your professional reputation aka your personal brand. Established networks can elevate you to positions of influence, allowing you to shape opinions, trends, and even policies within your industries.

Support system

- A professional network serves as a support system offering advice, feedback, and moral support, which is particularly beneficial during career transitions or challenging periods. Networking can result in partnerships or collaborations, where you can work together with other talented people to achieve common goals.

Networking benefits both the individuals and the organization. Today many organizations design workspaces to foster inter-departmental collaboration as it leads to enhancing business opportunities and facilitating knowledge transfer.

To emphasize, networking in the work context is about building a web of relationships that can provide a range of professional advantages, and it is an essential skill in the modern work environment where career paths are often non-linear, and where industries are rapidly evolving.

The Downsides of Not Networking

While networking is not the only path to professional success, its absence can create significant hurdles. The extent of these downsides can vary depending on the individual's industry, role, career stage, and personal style of working.

Limited career opportunities and growth

- Many job openings are not advertised and are filled through networking. Without a robust network, you may miss out on these opportunities. Internal promotions can often be influenced by who you know as much as what you know. Lack of networking might limit visibility with decision-makers.
- For entrepreneurs and freelancers, networking is crucial to finding new clients. Lack of networking can mean access to fewer business opportunities and partnerships. Networking often leads to mentorship opportunities. Without these relationships, you may lack guidance in navigating career challenges. Interacting with a diverse group of professionals can enhance personal qualities such as communication skills, empathy, and adaptability.

Narrow perspective

- A diverse network can be a great resource for problem-solving and brainstorming. Without it, you're limited to your own ideas and resources. Professional networks often provide emotional support and reassurance during challenging times. Lack of networking can lead to a sense of isolation, which may impact your confidence and self-esteem in professional settings.

Networking is usually an important facet of a successful career but isn't necessarily the be-all and end-all. The key is to find a balance and an approach that fits with your career goals and personal comfort level—the approach that feels genuine and comfortable to you.

Types of Networking

Let's take a look at different types of networking and their purposes.

Operational, personal, and strategic networking are three distinct but interrelated types of networking, each serving a different purpose and function in a professional context:

Operational Networking

- This is focused on getting things done efficiently and effectively within an organization. It involves building and maintaining relationships that help you fulfil your current job responsibilities. It typically includes connections with direct reports, superiors, and peers within your function, as well as other internal stakeholders who can influence or support your work. This can extend to key external stakeholders like suppliers, distributors, and customers.
- The primary goal of operational networking is to improve coordination and cooperation among those

involved in the day-to-day operations of a business. It's about creating a network that facilitates the smooth execution of tasks and projects.

Strategic Networking

- This is about forging relationships that help you navigate the broader complexities of organizational politics and the industry landscape. It's oriented towards future goals and strategic objectives. This type of networking typically involves connecting with higher-level professionals both within and outside one's organization. It may include other functional and business unit managers, industry leaders, and individuals who are not directly under one's control but are influential in the broader business context.
- The aim is to gain insight into the bigger picture of an organization or industry, understand strategic trends, and align one's career trajectory with these insights. It's about leveraging a network for advancement, influence, and access to resources beyond one's immediate control.

Personal Networking

- This is about creating and nurturing relationships outside of your immediate professional sphere. It often involves connecting with people based on shared personal interests, experiences, or backgrounds. These networks are largely external and are formed with individuals who may or may not be directly related to one's current job or industry. The connections are usually more informal and are based on mutual interests or hobbies.
- The focus here is on personal development and growth. Personal networking can provide diverse perspectives, support personal interests, and offer referral potential for future opportunities. One never knows how and when this network can also be valuable for career transitions or broadening one's horizons.

The preference and proficiency in operational, personal, or strategic networking can vary among women, depending on individual personalities, career stages, and the contexts in which they operate. Women are generally known for their strong collaborative and communication skills, which are key in operational networking. Their attention to detail and tendency towards inclusive management can make them adept at operational networking.

Inga Carboni—a professor at William & Mary's Mason School of Business—and her team did extensive research on how women improve their networks, the challenges they face, and what they and their organizations could do better. They found that most women's relationships, particularly those with female peers, are stickier than men's; growing stronger, more mutual, and more interwoven over time. Similar insights were shared by leadership consultant Sally Helgesen, who authored the book *How Women Rise* with Marshall Goldsmith. According to her, women tend to be comfortable with building close relationships, and may feel more at ease demonstrating warmth and concern for others.

Women often excel in personal networking due to their focus on building genuine, meaningful relationships. Their preference for quality over quantity in relationships can make personal networking particularly effective for women, as they often cultivate networks based on mutual trust and shared interests.

We understand that these observations are broad generalizations and may not apply to all women. However, we hope that some of these insights have resonated with our readers.

Each type of networking plays a critical role in professional development and career advancement, serving different needs and objectives at various stages of a professional journey. And when it comes to work related networking, a few characteristics stand out. They are all formal, structured, transactional in nature, and don't move into the realm of your personal life.

Place of Traditional Rules of Networking in Today's World

In a traditional context, networking is often perceived as something that one must indulge in a planned, structured, and formal way to build professional relationships that are specifically aimed at advancing one's career or business interests. Below, we will be discussing traditional forms of networking and will challenge them as well!

Formal and Structured

Events such as industry conferences, business luncheons, trade shows, and professional association meetings fall in the category of organized networking. The environment, dress codes, and context tend to be formal or business-like, reflective of the professional nature of the interactions. Typically, the exchange of business cards is a hallmark of traditional networking, symbolizing a formal introduction and the initiation of a professional relationship. This leads to people building both a literal and metaphorical 'Rolodex' of their contacts.

Since this form of networking is predominantly conducted in person, with a focus on physical meetings, internal events conducted within the organizations like conferences and training sessions also help with networking within employees from different functions or teams. These formal and structured ways of building your network still exist and work, however, they are no longer the only ways to grow your network.

Transactional in Nature

The primary goal of traditional networking is often to exchange information, seek job opportunities, or find potential clients. The interactions can sometimes be more about mutual benefit than personal connection. There's often an emphasis on connecting with individuals in higher positions, or with more industry influence, or with people from different organizations. Traditional networking might involve seeking mentors who are established in their fields, with a clear distinction between the mentor and mentee roles.

These types of networking forums still exist but have now evolved into specific communities getting together to support each other in their career and personal growth. For instance, there are many communities that are aimed at only women, C-level individuals, or women in senior leadership roles, providing them with a forum to connect with each other and benefit from each other's experience.

Professional Boundaries

Conversations in traditional networking settings typically focus on industry trends, career advice, or business opportunities. There is less emphasis on personal lives or external interests. There's usually a distinct boundary between professional networking and personal socializing. Post-event follow-up might include formal emails or phone calls, often with a specific agenda or proposal for further engagement.

Traditional networking can sometimes be seen as less flexible and more rigid, but it has been highly effective for many professionals and continues to be relevant, especially in certain industries and contexts like medical conferences, tech expos, etc.

Traditional networking events, unlike social gatherings, offer a lighter atmosphere where the pressure to form deep connections is lessened. This can be comforting for individuals who might typically feel overwhelmed in social settings. These events provide a low-key introduction to various professionals, allowing participants to explore potential connections at their own pace without the burden of forced interactions.

The evolution of networking doesn't necessarily replace traditional methods but rather expands the range of options available for professional relationship-building.

REWRITE THE RULES

With the new ways of working that have come into practice following the pandemic, it's a good time to challenge and relook at some of the old norms and establish new ones.

The traditional model of networking often suited men more than women. It may not fully resonate with some women leaders who prioritize building genuine relationships based on mutual benefit. Women may face unique challenges in networking, such as double standards for assertive behaviour and limited access to female role models, which can influence their approach to building professional connections.

For instance, the traditional emphasis on expanding one's network extensively is not the only approach to professional connections. Many women often prefer having fewer, deeper, and more meaningful connections as opposed to a larger number of contacts. It's important to recognize and respect the diverse ways in which people build their networks and understand that there is no one-size-fits-all approach to networking, and it's much better to use a more personalized and strategic approach that is tailored to individual preferences and specific needs and goals.

Some women leaders may be cautious about how their networking activities are perceived, because women may be judged more harshly for assertive networking behaviours often considered acceptable for men, leading to labels like 'pushy' or 'self-promotional'. Some women worry that networking can come off as disingenuous or manipulative. They may be uncomfortable with the transactional nature of some networking interactions, preferring meaningful connections over surface-level exchanges.

Certain industries are still very much male-dominated. Women might feel out of place or may not be included in informal networking opportunities, such as after-work gatherings. In some organizations/industries women may face implicit—or even explicit—biases that make networking more challenging. Women might perceive strategic networking opportunities as less accessible due to factors like informal networking happening in settings or at times that are less convenient or comfortable for them, such as after-hours social events.

Historically, networking has been dominated by male norms, leaving some women without readily available examples of successful female networkers. In general, women might be more cautious or less inclined towards certain aspects of strategic networking, particularly in environments that are not inclusive or where they face challenges due to gender dynamics. In many industries, especially at the higher levels of management, there's a lack of female representation. This can make strategic networking more daunting for women, as they might not see many role models or peers in these spaces.

One woman leader we spoke to clearly said that in the early part of her career she thought that she had to be more like men to succeed professionally, and this extended even to how she networked. It took her a long while to realize that to succeed you needed to be good at what you do and do that like a woman. She attributed this to not having any women role models to guide her during her early career days.

In addition to all the above, a combination of cultural, societal, and professional factors adds to the challenges faced by women in Asia when it comes to networking.

Traditional gender roles in many Asian societies often emphasize modesty and reserve for women, which can conflict with the proactive nature of networking. Women still bear the primary responsibility for childcare and household tasks, making it challenging to find time for networking activities, especially those outside of regular work hours.

Social and organizational hierarchies make some women feel uncomfortable reaching out to senior professionals or those in higher positions, which is often a key part of effective networking. These factors make networking a daunting task for many women, however, there are some who have worked with these challenges and created a network using their own approaches. Many women overcome these barriers and become exceptional networkers, often by adapting strategies that align with their own values and strengths.

Networking preferences and strengths can be influenced by a variety of factors, including individual personality, cultural background, industry norms, and personal experiences. For instance, introverts might prefer smaller, more intimate networking events where they can have deeper conversations, while extroverts might thrive in larger, high-energy settings. Or, having mentors or role models who excel at networking can influence an individual's approach and confidence in building professional connections.

Additionally, women's networking preferences and strengths can evolve as they progress in their careers and as workplace cultures become more inclusive and diverse. Through our conversations with several women leaders, we observed that many women leaders often go beyond mere transactional networking to build connections that are personal and strategic. We found that they are creating strong networks based on what feels genuine to them.

In fact, based on all the advice we heard from women leaders on networking, the mantra that stood out for us as the new rule is: Instead of building a network, build meaningful connections.

Here are some strategies that we garnered from the women leaders we spoke to on how to build 'strong connections':

- Engage authentically
- Foster connections
- Focus on quality over quantity
- Join networking platforms and forums

Engage Authentically

Many women leaders emphasized the importance of being authentic in their interactions. When they connect with other professionals, they focus not just on work related accomplishments but also on personal values, passions, and challenges. This helps create a strong foundation for a long-term relationship, as opposed to a transactional connection. They also bring 100 per cent of themselves into these connections and be their natural selves.

↔

Deepthi Bopaiah shared some great tips on accountability and follow through in building trust and credibility, the bedrock of authenticity, in one's network. Deepthi is the CEO of GoSports Foundation, a non-profit venture working to provide access to the ecosystem and to professionalize Indian sports. She is based in India and an avid sportsperson, and has represented her state, Karnataka, in tennis, and University in basketball. She is currently serving as a committee member on the Target Olympic Podium scheme of the Ministry of Youth affairs and Sports, India.

- Take the initiative to seek out mentors rather than waiting for them to approach you. Have the courage to start a conversation.
- Don't be deterred by rejection or a lack of response. Persistence and creativity in maintaining contacts pays dividends over time.
- When senior leaders offer to connect you to someone or provide advice, make sure to follow up with them. Or, if you committed to an action after meeting them, follow through. For example, if you discussed sharing a draft document or article with a leader after a networking meeting, actually send it rather than assume they won't have time or remember.
- Set calendar reminders and have discipline to close the feedback loop even with busy contacts to demonstrate reliability and build trust.
- Continually express gratitude and update your network on your progress so they feel invested in your growth.

Whether it is meeting a deadline, acknowledging advice, or showing you acted on recommendations, she believes executing on obligations made and not letting commitments slide forms the bedrock of productive professional relationships. Accountability and integrity in the little things make people confident in trusting you with bigger things.

↔

Foster Connections

We found that many women leaders we spoke to have the 'lift as you climb' mentality. They often engage in mutual support networks where the emphasis is on collective growth in the form of sharing resources, making introductions, or providing mentorship.

In writing this book, we were so heartened to see that women we spoke to recommended other women leaders to us to meet and talk. This was their way of acknowledging that there is something to learn from every woman's journey.

Ami Moris, retired CEO of MayBank Investment Banking Group, shared with us how participating in networking activities and being visible at events/forums did not come naturally to her, but she pushed herself because she realized visibility was crucial. She shared with us a set of questions she calls her 'social audit' and recommends always keeping these questions top of mind in order to identify and cultivate the relationships you need for sponsorship and advocacy. The key is focusing on who can open doors, vouch for you, provide honest feedback, navigate organizational politics, and influence decisions.

As Asian women, we face unique challenges in the workplace. We navigate expectations from both society and ourselves about how we should behave and lead. But here's the secret: You can have fun along the way!

While traditional networking often focuses on 'bro clubs', I believe in the power of sisterhood—a supportive network of women who encourage and sponsor each other. This goes beyond social gatherings; it's about having each other's backs, offering encouragement, and fostering sponsorship. Within these groups, you can learn to embrace fun and express your individuality.

Having sponsors, both male and female, is crucial. Sponsors are champions who vouch for you and your abilities. They help elevate your brand and advocate for your advancement. Hard work is essential, but in the boardroom, promotions rarely happen automatically. Networking ensures you're top-of-mind for those who can advocate for you.

To build a powerful network, conduct a regular 'social audit' by asking yourself these five questions:

1. **Who can introduce you to others?**
   Don't be afraid to ask people in your network for introductions. Their connections are valuable assets but be prepared for some resistance.

2. **Who can vouch for you?**
   Seek out sponsors, both inside and outside your organization, who can advocate for your skills and leadership potential.

3. **Who can give you candid feedback?**
   Surround yourself with people who offer honest feedback on your strengths and areas for improvement.

4. **Who can help you navigate organizational politics?**
   Understand the informal power dynamics within your organization. Identify the 'corridor powers' whose influence can impact your career.

5. **Who can help make things happen?**
   Recognize that those with decision-making authority may not always be readily apparent. Identify both internal and external stakeholders who can influence your career path.

By building a supportive network and conducting regular social audits, you can take control of your career trajectory. Don't wait for opportunities to come to you. Get out there, build connections, and have fun along the way!

↔

Women are frequently found to be more collaborative and community oriented. Networking that fosters a sense of support, collaboration, and mutual growth is often more appealing than competitive, transactional networking environments. Sometimes, sharing challenges or vulnerabilities can actually strengthen professional relationships. It can humanize leaders, make them more relatable, and create a space for genuine, meaningful conversations that go beyond shop talk.

Focus on Quality Over Quantity

Many of the women leaders we spoke to said that rather than focusing on accumulating a large number of connections, they aim for deeper relationships with fewer people. They invest time and effort in nurturing these relationships, turning connections into genuine friendships or partnerships.

Many women leaders are willing to invest in a relationship without expecting immediate returns. They value the organic development of the relationship and the mutual benefits that may arise over time. These women leaders also often engaged in building connections outside of the professional set up. They engage in forums that provide community service or social impact, or in groups that pertain to personal interests and hobbies. However, what is common to all these connections is that they are focused on cultivating strong meaningful connections.

↔

Nawan (Noom) Poovarawan, Director of Global Trust Service Delivery, Airbnb, shared with us how she approaches networking. She is currently based in Singapore and hails from Thailand. She has worked and lived in multiple countries including Japan, Thailand, and Singapore in Asia.

Noom believes that networking needs to align with one's personal values so it doesn't feel conflicting.

She leverages common interests/passions to find genuine connections rather than networking for its own sake. For instance, Noom has been building genuine support circles within fellow coaches' networks and has formed a peer coaching community. Another example is exchanging learning and new insights with people who share a common interest in the learning and development space.

She aims to build reciprocal relationships where she both provides and receives value. Rather than feeling the need to develop a vast network, she focuses on building an intimate, close-knit support circle that meets her needs.

Overall, Noom shared that it took time for her to build comfort with the idea of intentional relationship building, but she has been able to do it in an authentic way that supports her career.

↔

Join Networking Platforms and Forums

It'll be remiss to not talk about how technology is changing the way networking can take place. The traditional face-to-face methods of networking are being disrupted and augmented by technological advancements, societal shifts, and global events like the COVID-19 pandemic.

Younger women leaders are approaching networking with some distinct attributes, heavily influenced by digital technology, changing social norms, and an evolving understanding of leadership and diversity.

Professional networking platforms

- The rise of digital platforms has provided women with alternative networking avenues. It has never been easier to reach out to and connect with people using internet based professional networking platforms like LinkedIn, Shapr, and Opportunity.

- Social media and professional online networks can offer more controlled and comfortable environments for building connections. They tend to blend personal and professional identities online, giving a more well-rounded view of themselves. This approach often makes them more relatable and authentic in their networking efforts.
- Industry-specific forums like LinkedIn offer avenues to connect with professionals you might never meet otherwise. Webinars, virtual conferences, and Zoom meetups have replaced or supplemented physical events, especially post-pandemic as people have understood how to leverage these platforms better. It's much easier to discover, connect, and follow others who share your interests and build relationships with people in a community of your interest. You can also create and share valuable content via blogs, podcasts, or videos to attract a network interested in your expertise.

Community building

- Communities are a great source of support, wisdom, and guidance for women. Creating and being part of communities is a great way to build your network, and online forums and social media groups centred on common interests or challenges are becoming more common than before.
- Virtual spaces often allow for more diverse and inclusive networking opportunities, breaking down geographical and accessibility barriers. For many younger women leaders, networking isn't just about career advancement; it's also about connecting with people who share their values, such as social justice, environmental sustainability, or work–life balance.

Through our podcast *ReWrite The Rules* and this book, we are building a digital community across the region where emerging leaders can learn from the seasoned women leaders or women leaders who they identify with and network based on their interest. Seasoned leaders will get an opportunity to share their journeys and network with other leaders.

↔

The HRB article by Shawn Achor titled 'Do Women's Networking Events Move the Needle on Equality?' highlights that networking events facilitate building a sense of belonging and understanding of one's own worth for women. Women learn strategies for career advancement, fair pay, etc., from each other and not only find role models for themselves but also end up mentoring others.

By employing a mix of these strategies, women leaders can manage to go beyond mere networking to build connections that are both meaningful and enduring. This often translates into a robust support system that can be leveraged for mutual benefit over the long term.

These new methods allow for more personalized, value-driven, and equitable networking experiences. The new rules of networking are being reimagined—they are being re-written!

Multiplier Effect: 1 x 1 = ∞

Figure 3a

There were three distinct concepts that really stood out for us during our research on the topic of networking—boundary spanning, the strength of weak ties, and the five-minute favour.

Boundary Spanning

The term 'boundary spanning' was first introduced in organizational studies by Michael L. Tushman in the late 1970s to describe the ability of an individual or group to bridge the gap between different social groups, departments, or organizations. It involves effectively navigating and managing the different cultures, values, and norms of these groups in order to facilitate communication, collaboration, and knowledge exchange.

Boundary spanners are people that can help to break down silos, build relationships, and create a more inclusive and collaborative environment. They play a crucial role in fostering innovation, problem-solving, and organizational effectiveness.

In the context of networking and work, boundary spanners practise reaching out to and forming connections that go beyond one's immediate professional or social circles. They do this to build bridges between different groups, departments, disciplines, sectors, or even industries.

In today's world with more fluid careers where people move not only across functions but also industries, boundary spanning has more relevance.

The Strength of Weak Ties

The research by sociologist Mark Granovetter in his seminal paper titled 'The Strength of Weak Ties' emphasizes how even loose acquaintances can be valuable for career advancement. While this may seem counterintuitive to the idea of building close, meaningful connections, on reading Granovetter's work, we realized that even distant connections can sometimes be helpful. This is because weak ties connect you to circles outside of your own close network; they give you information that you wouldn't otherwise get.

For instance, you tell your close friends and family you're looking for a new job. They might be aware of some job openings but because they likely run in similar circles as you, the information they have about these jobs may be already known to you. However, you chat with an old college acquaintance on LinkedIn you haven't spoken to in a while. They work in a different industry and mention their company is hiring for a role that aligns with your skills. This weak tie provides fresh information you wouldn't have gotten from your close network.

This is the strength of weak ties. They bridge social circles and expose you to new ideas and opportunities you might otherwise miss.

Five-Minute Favour

The idea of a 'Five-minute Favour' was popularized by Adam Grant in his book *Give and Take: Why Helping Others Drives Our Success*. The five-minute favour is a practice of setting aside five minutes to help someone in your network without expecting anything in return. This could be an introduction, a recommendation, or even sharing an article.

Imagine you run into a colleague in the hallway who seems stressed about an upcoming presentation. A few examples of a five-minute favour in this scenario could be:

- **Offering to proofread a quick slide or two.** This small act takes minimal time from your day but can significantly ease your colleague's anxiety and ensure a polished presentation.
- **Sending a quick email introduction** connecting your colleague with someone in your network who might be relevant to their project.
- **Forwarding an interesting article** you came across that relates to your colleague's field of expertise.
- **Offering a listening ear** for a few minutes if your colleague needs to vent about a work challenge.

The key takeaway is that a five-minute favour is a small act of kindness that can have a big impact on someone else's day. It's about building relationships and fostering a culture of helping within your network.

Combining the research above, what we encourage you to do is to build your network one connection at a time. We're calling this the Multiplier Effect (*Figure 3a*).

The Multiplier Effect is about building genuine connections and offering value. Create the rules that work for you, be consistent in applying them, and that will lead you to cultivating a powerful network that opens doors to new opportunities and accelerates your career journey.

Here are some actions that you can take to multiply your network (*Figure 3b*):

Multiplier Effect: 1 x 1 = ∞

Map your existing network: Analyse your current connections across departments, disciplines, or industries. Look for gaps where you could build new connections.

Identify potential bridges: Look for opportunities to connect people from different groups within your network. This could involve introducing colleagues from different departments, connecting people with shared interests from different industries, or bridging the gap between your professional and personal networks.

Reach out to former colleagues and acquaintances: Reconnect with people you haven't spoken to in a while, even if it was just a brief interaction. A quick message can remind them of you and open doors for future collaboration.

Pay it forward: Encourage others in your network to practice the same principles, creating a ripple effect of connections and support.

★ **Be a good listener:** Actively listen to others in your network and learn about their needs and challenges. This will help you identify opportunities to connect them with others who can be of assistance.

Figure 3b

No One Way

As we have maintained through the earlier chapters, there is no one way of building your network. The idea is to be aware of the benefits and different approaches you can take, and then decide what feels authentic and comfortable to you.

↔

Let's consider two hypothetical women leaders, Grace and Siti, each with their own distinct networking styles. Their approaches reflect the diversity in how individuals can navigate building and maintaining professional relationships.

NETWORKING STYLES

Grace's Networking Style: The Relationship Builder

Emphasis on deep connections

- Grace believes in forming deep, meaningful relationships. She prefers having a smaller, tightly knit network where she knows each person well.

Quality over quantity

- Instead of attending every networking event, Grace chooses selectively, focusing on gatherings where she can have in-depth conversations.

Follow-up

- After meeting someone new, Grace always follows up with a personalized message, referencing specific points from their conversation.

Mentorship focus

- She actively seeks to mentor others and often reaches out to junior colleagues or professionals, offering guidance and support.

Holistic approach

- Grace's networking isn't just professional; she engages with her connections on a personal level, showing interest in their hobbies, families, and personal achievements.

Selective use of social media

- She uses platforms like LinkedIn thoughtfully, sharing articles and posts that resonate with her values and professional ethos.

Siti's Networking Style: The Strategic Connector

Broad and diverse network

- Siti's approach is to have a wide-ranging network across various industries and professions. She believes in the power of diverse connections.

Active online presence

- Siti is very active on professional social networks. She regularly shares industry insights, comments on others' posts, and engages in professional groups.

Event networking

- She attends many events and is skilled at initiating conversations with new people, often leaving with several new connections.

Strategic relationships

- Siti often thinks strategically about whom to connect with, focusing on potential mutual benefits and opportunities.

Leveraging Connections

- Siti is adept at connecting people in her network with each other, facilitating introductions and collaborations.

Regular check-ins

- Siti maintains her broad network by periodically checking in with her connections, often through quick messages or comments on social media.

ANALYSIS

When we look closely at both Grace and Siti's style we see that there are some differences:

- **Depth vs. Breadth:** Grace's style is about depth and meaningful connections, while Siti focuses on breadth and strategic positioning.
- **Personal vs. Professional:** Grace blends the lines between personal and professional, whereas Siti maintains a more professional focus.
- **Mentorship vs. Mutuality:** Grace is driven by a desire to mentor and guide, while Siti seeks mutually beneficial relationships.

Both Grace and Siti are effective networkers, but their methods and priorities differ significantly. Grace's style is beneficial for building a supportive and deeply engaged network, while Siti's approach is excellent for creating a wide-reaching network that offers diverse opportunities and insights. These contrasting styles illustrate that there's no one-size-fits-all approach to networking; it's about what aligns best with one's personality and style.

Let's see both the styles in action at the Annual Industry Conference—a regional conference in Kuala Lumpur attended by about 1000 people from over twelve countries.

AT THE ANNUAL INDUSTRY CONFERENCE

GRACE'S APPROACH

Grace enters the conference hall with a calm demeanour. She's already researched a few attendees she wants to connect with—individuals whose values align with hers and who could be potential long-term collaborators.

During the coffee break, she spots Anna, a young entrepreneur she's been following on LinkedIn. Grace approaches her, complimenting Anna on a recent article she wrote. They delve into a deep conversation about industry trends and challenges. Grace listens intently, sharing her own experiences and offering insights.

Later, during a panel discussion, Grace asks thoughtful questions that spark a lively debate. After the session, she stays back to chat with the panellists, building rapport. As the conference wraps up, Grace has added a few significant contacts to her network. She plans to follow up with a personalized email, maybe even suggesting a one-on-one meeting to explore mutual interests.

SITI'S APPROACH

Siti arrives at the conference with a clear strategy. Her goal is to meet as many relevant people as possible and to establish a broad range of contacts.

She's quick to introduce herself, efficiently exchanging business cards and moving from one conversation to the next. During the networking session, Siti skilfully navigates the room, joining various groups, sharing her insights, and learning about others' work. She's adept at identifying potential synergies and suggesting future collaborations.

Siti uses her social media savviness to her advantage, live-tweeting the event and connecting with attendees online in real-time. By the end of the day, her LinkedIn network has grown substantially, and she has several leads to follow up on.

AT THE END OF THE DAY

Grace leaves the conference feeling content. She has made meaningful connections and looks forward to building these relationships further. Her approach is about quality and depth.

Siti, energized by her new connections, is already planning follow-up messages and setting reminders to touch base with her new contacts. Her approach is about quantity and breadth.

REFLECTION

In the story above, Grace and Siti exemplify two distinct networking philosophies. Grace's strategy is about forming deep, lasting connections with a few individuals, while Siti's approach is to cast a wide net and establish a diverse range of contacts.

Both methods have their strengths—Grace's approach leads to strong, trust-based relationships, beneficial for long-term collaborations and support. Siti's strategy creates a vast network, providing diverse opportunities and a wide range of resources and ideas.

Their styles show that effective networking can vary greatly depending on one's personality, goals, and preferred way of interacting with others.

SUMMARY

Importance of networking: Networking is a long-term investment that yields significant returns. By actively building genuine connections, offering value, and fostering collaboration, you create a powerful network that empowers you to thrive in your career.

Types of Networking

- **Strategic networking:** Create connections with key influencers to understand industry shifts, advance your career, and secure resources beyond your reach. This is networking for impact, not just connections.
- **Operational networking:** Cultivate relationships that fuel your current role, connecting with team, bosses, and beyond to get the job done smoothly. Build a network that makes everyday tasks and projects effortless through internal and external partnerships.
- **Personal networking:** Nurture connections outside your professional sphere to explore new interests, gain support, and unlock future possibilities.

Multiplier Effect—grow your network exponentially

- **Map your existing network.** Analyse your current connections across departments, disciplines, or industries, and look for gaps that you can bridge.
- **Reach out to former colleagues and acquaintances.** Reconnect with people you haven't spoken to in a while. A quick message can remind them of you and open doors for future collaboration.
- **Identify potential bridges.** Look for opportunities to connect people from different groups within your network.

- **Pay it forward.** Encourage others in your network to practise the same principles, creating a ripple effect of connections and support.
- **Be a good listener.** Actively listen to others in your network and learn about their needs and challenges.

REFLECT: SELF-ASSESS: ACTION

Reflect what we just discussed in the chapter above and use the following four blockers to **self-assess** where you are on the networking journey and write out one **action** that you can take to build your network.

Sustain	Shrink
What behaviours should you continue to practice? Positive behaviours that are working well for you. For example, being part of a professional community or an active member of your college alumni.	What behaviours are not serving you well in networking? Habits that you want to see less of. For example, forgetting to follow up after a conversation.
The behaviours I want to sustain are . . . _____ _____ _____ _____	The behaviours I want to shrink are . . . _____ _____ _____ _____

Discard	Amplify
What is not working well for you? Getting rid of mindsets that aren't working for you at all. For example, getting rid of the mindset that networking is only transactional.	What behaviours that you currently demonstrate need to be practised more? Practices that you should do more of. For example, connecting people from different parts of your network.
The behaviours I want to discard are . . .	The behaviours I want to amplify are . . .
_____ _____ _____ _____	_____ _____ _____ _____

Some bonus questions to ask yourself to assess the quality of your network and networking habits:

1. Do I have a diverse network?
2. Am I too focused on quantity over quality, or vice versa?
3. Am I proactive in maintaining my connections?
4. Do I offer value in my networking relationships?
5. Am I utilizing online and offline networking effectively?
6. Is my networking primarily transactional or relational?
7. Do I follow up after the initial interaction?

Take Action

- What is your one practice that you will put into action to build your connections?

4

The Achieving Balance Rule

The phrase 'work–life balance' in the context of women in the workplace always conjures up the image of a woman juggling work, family, home. Media is full of memes, cartoons, and pictures depicting that image of balance in an uncomplimentary way, blatantly calling out that it's only a woman's job to fulfil these multiple roles.

We want to rewrite that unspoken (and sometimes spoken) rule.

Before we dive into the conversation on balance, here is a funny anecdote that showcases the biases that influence it.

↔

Ritu's Story

I was working on a project with some senior executives of a private bank. The project required me to travel extensively, and I was in Thailand for a meeting. One day, over a power lunch a senior executive, amidst discussions of market trends, turned to me and asked, 'Ritu, who takes care of your kids when you travel?' My smile faltered and a familiar irritation bubbled up. I took a deep breath, and instead of laughing the comment off, I said, 'Well, they do have a father, you know.' The gentleman, thankfully, understood the unspoken message.

This wasn't the first time I'd faced this question. Throughout my career, it's become a recurring theme, a subtle reminder of the invisible tightrope working mothers often walk. My husband, however, has never been asked similar questions.

The story above showcases that stark disparity of the weight carried by many mothers in the professional world. The story isn't about shaming or blaming anyone, but about acknowledging the unspoken assumption that childcare falls primarily on mothers' shoulders. It's about sparking conversations, fostering empathy, and pushing towards a more equitable future where work and family responsibilities are shared, not solely borne by one parent.

↔

Even if you are not a parent, women in general are asked questions in a similar vein about balancing family responsibilities with working.

As we navigate this balancing act, let's start with defining balance.

We know that the importance and benefits of balance are obvious, and everyone seems to know them. Yet, we find ourselves struggling with it. There is a small step between knowing and doing! So, we thought a bit of stating the obvious, a reminder won't hurt.

The definition of balance is broad and varied reflecting its multifaceted nature. In some places it is referred to as a physical equilibrium, and other times it is about having the right amount—not too much or too little of anything. Balance involves situations where different things exist in equal, correct, or right amounts.

Applying these definitions to the concept of work–life balance, we see it as an integration of various aspects of one's life rather than the traditional binary approach to work–life balance that segregates time spent in office from the time spent on other things in one's life. A balanced life integrates work with your personal priorities and passions—family, hobbies, and self-care.

While the concept of balance will vary greatly depending on individual circumstances and cultural contexts, its pursuit is generally seen as a cornerstone of a healthy, fulfilling life. One needs to find the right equilibrium that allows for personal and professional growth without compromising on health and happiness.

Rajita, drawing on her medical background, correlated balance with the concept of homeostasis—the body's remarkable ability to maintain equilibrium despite external changes. This principle, crucial for survival, applies equally to life. Just as imbalances in the body lead to physical disorders, imbalances in life lead to burnout, stress, and decreased well-being.

Think of your life as a complex system, where neglecting one aspect throws off others. Chronic sleep deprivation, for example, impacts work productivity and focus. Achieving balance, like homeostasis, requires constant adjustments—adapting priorities, time, and resources to ever-changing circumstances.

Self-reflection and feedback loops, similar to the body's monitoring systems, help us assess our current state of balance and make necessary adjustments. Remember, balance isn't about achieving perfection, but rather a holistic approach to managing work, family, personal growth, and relaxation.

Just as homeostasis is vital for physical health, a balanced life is crucial for overall well-being—encompassing mental, emotional, and physical health. Both our bodies and our lives require constant work—maintaining stability, adapting to change, and striving for optimal conditions for healthy functioning.

In essence, like our bodies, our lives require constant work to maintain stability, adapt to change, and function optimally. Knowing what you need to do to achieve balance is key. And one thing is for certain, a lack of balance in one area of your life impacts every other aspect as well.

Different Kinds of Balance

Achieving balance is a dynamic and ongoing process. It requires self-awareness, adaptability, and sometimes the courage to challenge conventional norms.

Whether it is looking at short-term needs versus long-term goals, understanding when to take risks versus when to maintain stability, or effectively managing time, energy, and resources, balance is prioritizing tasks and commitments to ensure that important areas of life and work receive adequate attention.

Given that there are many facets to balance, we've tried to categorize the different dimensions of balance as follows:

Mental and Emotional Balance

- Managing and regulating emotions is crucial for overall well-being. Emotional balance involves understanding and appropriately responding to one's emotional states, and coping with stress, anxiety, and other emotional challenges. Maintaining a healthy state of mind through intellectual stimulation, critical thinking, and mindfulness is also important. Mental balance can be achieved by keeping the mind active and engaged, but also allowing time for mental rest and relaxation.
- Beyond the daily grind of work tasks, mental balance can also include investing time in learning new skills, career planning, and personal professional growth.

Physical Balance

- Apart from the typical focus on exercise and diet, physical balance also involves understanding and responding to the body's needs, such as taking adequate rest, getting enough sleep, indulging in a physical activity, and timely medical care. Physical balance can include listening to the body and maintaining physical health in a holistic manner.

Social Balance

- Balancing social interactions involves maintaining healthy and fulfilling relationships while also ensuring personal space and time. It is also important to build social connections and contribute to one's cultural and social community in a way that aligns with one's values. This aspect of social balance is more specific and valuable to the Asian cultural context. This helps with having a more rounded perspective to life and as we've seen earlier, social connections contribute to our emotional well-being.

In a dynamic world with economic and environmental uncertainties, recognizing how the different types of balance are intertwined empowers you to take a holistic approach towards finding what works best for you. This will look different for different people depending on the stage of life, career, and interest. Finding balance in different aspects of your life makes it more fulfilling where everything feels connected and supported.

Achieving Balance for Women

For Asian women leaders, the approach to achieving balance is more complex. Balance for them is not just about equal distribution of time or resources but also involves making choices that align with values and goals in the Asian cultural context, personally and at the workplace.

Cultural Expectations

In many Asian cultures, there are deeply ingrained gender expectations. For instance, women are often expected to prioritize family and household responsibilities like taking care of the elderly or young children, regardless of their professional status. This cultural norm can create significant pressure to fulfil dual roles perfectly, leading to feeling overwhelmed, stressed, and a feeling of being stretched too thin.

Women who prioritize their careers can face social stigma or be labelled negatively, which can add emotional and mental strain. It makes it difficult to find a personal sense of balance.

Some women often put a self-imposed pressure on themselves to excel in every aspect of life. This can lead to unrealistic expectations and a sense of never doing enough, which makes it hard to have a sense of balance. This often stems from personal aspirations or societal expectations where self-care may be perceived as being selfish, leading to a propensity to overwork and neglect personal well-being.

As life evolves through different stages and milestones like motherhood, marriage, and family, the pressure to fulfil self-imposed or societal expectations without prioritizing personal needs creates an imbalance.

Workplace Gender Bias

Despite progress in some areas, gender bias still exists in many workplaces. Career breaks due to childbirth, child-rearing, and care-giving can impact career progression for women and make it challenging to maintain a balance between personal and professional aspirations.

Although this is now changing, traditionally, many Asian workplaces have been slow to adopt flexible work arrangements that could help women better balance their responsibilities. The concept of work–life balance can be particularly challenging in the Asian context, where work cultures often demand long hours and high levels of commitment. For instance, for women with dual roles as caregivers and professionals, this lack of support can create a significant barrier to career advancement.

Limited Support Networks

Support networks both at work and outside of work are equally important. As discussed in our previous chapter on connections, women may have less access to supportive professional networks which are crucial for career growth and balance. This manifests itself in the form of fewer women in leadership positions to serve as mentors and role models, or a lack of support networks specifically geared towards women and their challenges.

The lack of access to supportive networks or resources outside of work such as childcare, eldercare, or flexible work arrangements too makes achieving balance significantly more difficult.

These challenges require not only personal resilience and adaptability from women leaders but also systemic changes in workplaces and societies to support a more balanced approach to work and life. Through this book our hope is to not only highlight what women can do personally, but also in terms of creating systemic change, how they can advocate for themselves and actively seek support from their organizations.

Achieving balance in life can be challenging due to a variety of factors, which often intertwine and influence each other. As people move through different stages of life, their priorities and responsibilities change, requiring constant readjustment in the pursuit of balance. What works at one stage may not be suitable for another.

The solution lies in managing these external and internal factors effectively, while also being adaptable to life's changing circumstances. It requires self-awareness, setting realistic expectations, and sometimes, the courage to prioritize and make tough choices that align with one's values and needs.

In our conversations with Asian women leaders, we asked them what balance means to them. Their answers varied based on individual experiences, cultural backgrounds, and personal values. They showcase the unique challenges that are a combination of cultural, societal, and professional factors we outlined above.

Some common themes emerged in how they conceptualize and strive for balance:

Juggling multiple roles

- Many women leaders described balance as the ability to effectively juggle multiple roles: as professionals, mothers, partners, daughters, friends, and community members.

- For them, it is all about allocating time and energy across the various aspects of their lives that are important to them and doing it in a way that feels fulfilling and sustainable. They felt that approaching their circumstances with flexibility and adaptability helped them respond to the change really well. This could mean being able to adjust work schedules to accommodate personal needs, or vice versa, or finding ways to be able to support either work or family in the face of unexpected challenges.
- Many quoted having an equitable partnership with their partners or other family members where household and childcare responsibilities are shared, allowing women to pursue their careers and personal interests more freely.

Personal fulfilment

- For many women leaders, achieving balance isn't just about juggling responsibilities, it's deeply linked to their personal fulfilment and happiness. Carving out time for activities, hobbies, and passion projects that hold personal meaning brings them joy and satisfaction beyond their professional accomplishments. These pursuits often address their need for maintaining physical health, finding mental and emotional well-being, and even pursuing spiritual fulfilment. This creates a sense of wholeness that fuels their overall success and vitality.
- Self-care is another critical aspect of balance for many women leaders. This isn't just about bubble baths and face masks (although those can be helpful too!) but about actively prioritizing activities that nourish their well-being and replenish their energy through regular exercise, meditation, etc.
- By prioritizing these holistic aspects of well-being, these women leaders were cultivating a more sustainable and fulfilling leadership style. They said they feel better

equipped to navigate the demands of their roles while maintaining their personal happiness and well-being.

Feeling of control

- Balance is often equated with a sense of control over one's life. It's the feeling that they are making deliberate choices about how they spend their time and energy, rather than being constantly reactive to external demands. Many women talk about balance in terms of setting and maintaining boundaries between work and personal life.

- The common thread was about being in control and making deliberate choices. While it sounds simple, it is easier said than done and so, we see that there is so much conversation about it.

- The specific activities and strategies that contribute to balance will vary depending on each individual's unique needs and preferences. The key takeaway is that achieving balance is a journey, not a destination. It's about finding what works for you and actively nurturing your well-being in all its dimensions.

↔

Our conversation with Meera Vasudevan, co-founder, C-SAW (Center for the Spread of Affordable Wellness), Singapore, showcased how women's expectations of balance and success have dramatically shifted over time. Meera has lived in India, America, and Singapore.

For a long time, society told us 'balance' meant being a perfect wife, mother, and homemaker. Many women dedicated themselves to that path, but some felt disillusioned later, realizing they'd been pushed onto a 'mommy track' without their true desires considered.

The pressure then shifted to juggling a demanding career alongside family life, this 'superwoman' ideal. While admirable, it led many to burnout and exhaustion. The message of 'leaning in' only added to the burden, ignoring the real struggles and limitations we face.

But today, women are reclaiming their narratives. We're rejecting the one-size-fits-all approach and instead, defining success on our own terms. It might be excelling in a chosen profession, prioritizing personal fulfilment, or simply being a good human being. We may choose marriage, family, a single life, or something else entirely—it's up to us.

The point is that we're no longer beholden to external definitions. We're striving for individual goals and celebrating each other's unique journeys. And we're calling for a society that finally lets women define success as they like, just like men have always been able to.

Ultimately, I believe women have made incredible strides in challenging restrictive ideas. But the fight isn't over. We need to keep working towards a world where women are empowered to choose their own paths and be celebrated for who they truly are.

Why Focus on Balance Is Important

Achieving balance isn't always easy. Companies often default to the 'always on' mentality, but it's our responsibility to advocate for ourselves because balance isn't just a perk, it's a necessity. It's the difference between feeling energized and engaged or burned out and resentful.

Here are some areas that benefit directly from bringing balance in your life:

Productivity and Sustainability

- Maintaining a balance helps in preventing burnout, stress, and physical exhaustion. When you focus on balance, you allow yourself adequate rest and recuperation which are essential for long-term physical health and mental well-being. People who manage a healthy balance between different aspects of their lives often demonstrate higher productivity and performance in their professional and personal endeavours. When not overburdened by one aspect of life, individuals can focus better and bring more energy and creativity to their tasks.

Improved Relationships

- A balanced life allows for quality time with family and friends which is crucial for nurturing strong, supportive relationships. It helps in building a solid support system that is vital for personal happiness and overcoming life's challenges. When individuals maintain a balanced life, they are often better positioned to contribute positively to society whether through work, community service, or simply by setting a positive example by having a more holistic and rich life.

Personal Fulfilment and Growth

- Focus on balance enables individuals to pursue varied interests and passions, contributing to a more fulfilling and enriched life. Engaging in diverse activities can lead to greater personal satisfaction and a sense of accomplishment. Balancing different aspects of life can lead to self-discovery, personal growth, and a deeper understanding of one's values and priorities. Balance is key to sustainable living. Without it, individuals might achieve short-term success at the expense of long-term health and happiness.

Traditional Rules of Balance

The word 'balance' is thrown around so much that it's become a cliché. But beneath the buzzword, there are hidden myths that distort its true meaning.

Historically, the traditional rules for balance, particularly as they apply to women, have been shaped by societal norms and cultural expectations. These rules, while varying across different cultures and communities, typically emphasized conventional gender roles and often placed restrictive boundaries on women's personal and professional lives.

One-Size-Fits-All Approach

This implies that there is a universal standard of what balance should look like and that it should work for everybody. However, balance looks different for different people and is influenced by the individual's life circumstances, priorities, and definitions of success.

For example, most people think that work needs to be accomplished within the allotted eight hours every day, typically from 9 a.m. to 5 p.m. This was true in the days when we worked with people in the same time zone, region, and when we didn't have the technology to take work home.

Balance Is Solely an Individual Responsibility

Traditionally, the onus of achieving balance in one's life lay entirely on the individual. However, organizational policies, societal norms, and support systems all play a crucial role in facilitating or hindering a balanced life.

Traditionally, women were expected to prioritize family responsibilities over professional ambitions. The idea of a successful woman was often tied more to her roles as a mother, wife, and homemaker, rather than as a career professional or leader. If women were working, they were often encouraged to pursue careers only until they reached a certain life milestone, such as marriage or childbirth, after which their primary focus was expected to shift to family. Women were and often still are expected to be the primary caregivers in families, responsible not only for physical caregiving but also for the emotional well-being of family members.

Taking Time for Self Is Selfish

Some people believe that women prioritizing self-care or making time for personal interests is selfish especially when they have family or work responsibilities. There's often an assumption that working longer hours demonstrates more commitment to one's job and being more productive. Traditionally, sacrifice is seen as a virtue in personal or professional lives. The notion that women should be willing to sacrifice their own needs, aspirations, and well-being for the sake of their family or others has been a prevalent old rule. Self-care and personal ambitions were often seen as secondary.

Equal Balance Is Always Achievable/ You Can Have It All

Traditionally, people approach balance by hoping to simultaneously excel in all aspects of life: career, family, personal health, and hobbies, with equal intensity and success. However, balance often requires trade-offs and prioritizing different aspects at different times. Additionally, working towards a balanced work life is often perceived as a lack of commitment or ambition in one's career.

While these traditional rules have significantly influenced the lives of many women, luckily there's a growing shift in attitudes and practices. This shift is crucial in empowering women to define and achieve their own sense of balance and break free from outdated norms and expectations.

The Guilt Factor

Looking back, mother's guilt was a huge thing for me in those early days. Back then, fathers didn't have the long paternity leave they do now, which is fantastic. My husband stayed home for a while, but then went back to work. I only took a month off, when the norm was three, and then I rushed back in.

Of course, I felt guilty. Guilty for wanting to go back to work, guilty for needing that space, and especially guilty for finding some level of fulfilment and happiness away from my children. My husband just didn't understand at that time. Society told him, and me, that mothers are supposed to be happy just being with their kids. 'Look at the happy mom and child,' right?

But the truth is, I deeply valued my time at work. It wasn't just about escaping, it shaped how my children see the world and what women can be. It was tough, though. Why was I pressuring myself so much?

Even now, travelling for work brings tears. Leaving my kids is always hard. Yet, when I'm immersed in my work and doing well, a different kind of happiness takes over. It's a different kind of fulfilment, and it's important to me too.

This experience taught me that the 'perfect' balance doesn't exist. It's a constant dance between different needs and emotions, and that's okay. Both motherhood and my career give me joy, even if it comes with a sprinkle of tears sometimes.

This anecdote above is shared by Nora Nazerene Abu Bakar, vice president and publisher, Penguin Random House SEA. She is based in Singapore and comes with extensive experience in the publishing industry across Asia. Her story is an example of that one word that we constantly heard from several women through our research and interviews when we spoke about balance. Guilt.

Guilt when they spent time away from their children, guilt when they prioritized themselves over others, guilt when they had to say no to their bosses.

In talking to some of our male colleagues, we realized that this guilt factor is (more) specific to women. The guilt factor that many women experience when spending time on themselves (and their career) is a significant psychological barrier, deeply rooted in societal norms and traditional gender roles.

From a young age, many women are culturally conditioned to be caregivers, often placing others' needs before their own.

Society imposes high standards on women, expecting them to excel in all roles as professionals, mothers, partners, and homemakers. Traditional gender roles often dictate that a woman's primary responsibility is to others. All this leads to feelings of guilt when they prioritize themselves.

This guilt shows up in many ways and impacts women negatively.

Women might neglect their own health and well-being, considering it less important than their roles and responsibilities towards others. There may be reluctance to invest time in personal interests, hobbies, or professional development due to feeling that such activities are selfish. The guilt of taking time for themselves can contribute to chronic stress and burnout, as they continuously overextend to meet expected obligations.

The way to overcome this guilt starts with writing the rules about what is expected of us and what we need to thrive. It's essential to reframe self-care and personal time as not only beneficial but necessary for overall well-being and effectiveness in other life roles. Recognizing one's own worth and understanding that self-care is a right, not a privilege, is crucial.

Learning to set and maintain healthy boundaries is key. It's about understanding that saying no or taking time for oneself is not neglectful but a part of self-preservation. We will talk more about boundaries later in the chapter.

Building a supportive network that helps to validate the importance of personal time can help in mitigating feelings of guilt. Societal shifts in redefining gender roles to be more inclusive and equitable can help reduce the guilt associated with self-prioritization. Overcoming the guilt associated with self-prioritization is crucial for the mental, emotional, and physical well-being of women. It involves a combination of personal mindset shifts and broader societal changes.

By addressing this guilt, women can move towards a more balanced, fulfilling life where their own needs are valued and attended to.

REWRITE THE RULES

In a world where we work with colleagues across multiple time zones and take work back home on our laptops and phones, the lines between offices and homes are blurred. Therefore, women today are approaching balance differently thus creating new and innovative rules to lead more fulfilling lives. These rules reflect a shift towards greater self-awareness, holistic well-being, and challenging traditional norms. For some these rules were rewritten because of life events like childbirth and health issues, and for others due to a harsh wakeup call like falling asleep behind the wheel of their car while driving or death of a close friend or colleague.

We've picked a few that were recurrent themes in our interviews with the Asian women leaders we spoke to.

Prioritizing Self-Care

Women are recognizing that self-care is essential for sustained performance. Taking time for yourself, to invest in your physical, mental, and emotional well-being is important. Also important is making time for hobbies, upskilling, or other passion projects that replenish your energy levels. This includes getting adequate rest, engaging in physical activities, mindful practices like meditation, and seeking professional help when needed. So many women leaders we spoke to said that they are making time for activities and hobbies that bring joy and relaxation, which is crucial for mental and emotional rejuvenation.

↔

For instance, this experience that Professor Sun Sun Lim—vice president of Partnerships & Engagement, Singapore Management University—shared with us, struck a chord with us on how important prioritizing personal health is.

Sometimes, when we're juggling multiple commitments, we feel pressure to pour our best into everything: our jobs, our families, our relationships. But the reality is, we can't give our best to others unless we give our best to ourselves.

My schedule gets pretty hectic—meeting industry partners, hosting university visits, travelling to speak at conferences, serving on academic and industry committees, writing my research articles and op-eds . . . the list goes on. So, at the beginning of each week, I block out time for the gym in my calendar, usually every other evening. Treating it like a non-negotiable appointment ensures I actually go and don't get sidetracked by other meetings.

This gym time is more than just physical activity; it's my self-care hack. I catch up on podcasts, reflect without staring at a screen, and simply be present with myself. This dedication to health has been transformative. Exercise boosts my energy, improves my sleep, and keeps me sharp overall.

Finding balance wasn't always easy. When my children were younger, things were hectic. Now that they're teenagers and more independent, attending networking events or hitting the gym after dinner is much smoother. So, to my younger counterparts: It gets easier! You become more confident and settled in your career, and your family dynamics should stabilize over time.

Remember, taking care of yourself isn't selfish, it's essential. You can't pour from an empty cup. By prioritizing your well-being, you'll be better equipped to give your all to everything and everyone else in your life.

↔

Flexible Work Schedules

More and more women leaders are embracing flexible working hours and remote work opportunities to better manage professional and personal responsibilities. While in the past the segregation of time for work and life worked alright, in today's globally connected work environments it's hard to draw boundaries on when work ends, and life begins. However, with technology tools that help with communication, remote collaboration, and planning, it's easier to adapt to an approach that is flexible.

↔

Here is what Nawan (Noom) Poovarawan—director of Global Trust Service Delivery, Airbnb, Singapore—shared with us when we asked her how she balances her schedule to make time for all her hobbies and work.

Juggling work, personal interests, and a demanding global role can feel like a constant balancing act. While I have other passions like dancing, ikebana, and poetry, I recognize that work holds a significant place in my life. Instead of aiming for traditional work–life balance, I strive for work–life integration, where both aspects contribute to a fulfilling whole.

This requires adjustments, and initially, I had to calibrate my effort level to fit the global role where I was running a global operations team that spans across LATAM, US, Ireland, Singapore, and India with headquarters in the US. I had to ensure it benefits the business, the team, and myself. This involved:

Protecting energizing activities outside work

- While how I 'protect' this time might differ in my new role, identifying activities like Pilates, Yoga, lunch with friends, peer coaching, and attending courses/ workshops, and scheduling them remains crucial. These activities give me energy.

Managing personal well-being

- Adapting to different time zones and ensuring sufficient rest are essential for sustained performance.

Setting clear boundaries

- The 'work hard, play hard' mentality applies, but it's crucial to define expectations for both myself and others. Saying 'no' firmly becomes more important, even if it challenges my tendency to accommodate.

This last point, drawing boundaries, is the hardest part. Saying no, especially in a global role, feels counterintuitive. But I've learned to trust my instincts, knowing that sometimes saying yes leads to regret, while clear boundaries bring relief.

Just yesterday, I requested to reschedule a meeting that usually takes place past midnight my time. This meeting has over twenty-five attendees and I am the only one from Singapore. Given its global nature, it's really hard to find a time zone that fits all calendars, so the meeting ends up in the time zone that is convenient for the majority of participants.

Normally, I would watch the recorded meeting. However, this time there was an aspect of the agenda for which I wanted to be there real time and participate actively. Hence, I requested a change in the meeting time to accommodate my time zone despite the inconvenience to others.

It's okay to adjust our approach based on evolving needs and understanding. Sometimes, recordings suffice, but other times, real-time engagement is essential. This constant learning and adaptation are key to navigating the complexities of work–life integration, especially in demanding roles.

↔

Learning To Say No

Like Noom mentioned above, women leaders are now becoming assertive in setting and communicating boundaries to protect their time and energy. This includes saying no to excessive workloads and ensuring personal time is respected. Being clear and assertive about needs and limitations in both personal and professional settings.

↔

Fanny Huang—VP Strategic Deals and Head of ESG APAC, at DHL Supply Chain—shared how being very clear about your boundaries, respecting them yourself, and adhering to them are key to focusing on what matters to you.

> Managing dependencies, especially as women, often requires a mix of strategies. Having a routine is key, even if it involves a bit of 'militaristic' planning. Setting boundaries becomes crucial, particularly in high-travel roles. In my case, I am very clear about when I can travel and when I cannot.
>
> Speaking up when boundaries are challenged is equally important. We often compartmentalize work and personal life, but the reality is they blur. Traditional Asian work ethics, with long hours and prioritizing work above all else, are shifting, even in Singapore.
>
> I'm fortunate to work at DHL, where we embrace a 'respect and results' culture. While results naturally matter for any business, respect for personal boundaries, family time, and overall well-being is equally valued.

Finding an organization that partners with you to achieve this balance is crucial.

As female leaders, we set an example for others around us. It's our responsibility to showcase balance and encourage others to find their own. We may not see ourselves as role models, but our actions resonate with those around us, especially younger women. Finding your voice is easier when you see leaders embodying a healthy work–life balance.

I like to use the analogy of driving. There are times in life when you press the accelerator, seeking speed and momentum. But there are also periods when you need to slow down, navigate a crowded road, or even walk altogether.

It's perfectly ok to slow down when we need to, and we shouldn't feel like we have failed. The key is to remain in control of the pace, knowing when to push and when to release the accelerator when we want to. Finding this balance allows you to navigate different seasons of life while maintaining an overall sense of harmony.

↔

As mentioned in our last chapter, in addition to these new rules, women leaders are leaning heavily on the support of other women leaders who have either walked the same journey or are facing similar challenges with balance. Women leaders are focusing on creating and maintaining networks of support, both professionally and personally. They are also leaning on delegating tasks at work for sharper focus and outsourcing domestic responsibilities, when possible, to create more space for personal priorities.

We are seeing that women are also redefining what success means to them. We will spend a considerable time discussing that in the next chapter but, suffice to say, that in the context of balance, the definition of success now includes personal well-being and happiness, rather than just professional achievements and societal expectations. They are prioritizing what matters most at different times. Women leaders are now continuously seeking personal growth opportunities.

By adopting these new rules women are challenging conventional norms and carving out paths that lead to more balanced, fulfilling lives. They are pushing for and utilizing policies that support working parents, such as parental leave, flexible childcare options, and caregiver support.

These approaches emphasize the importance of individual well-being as a critical component to overall life satisfaction and effectiveness in any role.

Boundary Setting

Setting boundaries is not easy. Most people find it hard to say no to things that they don't want to spend their time and energy on. In the Asian context, we find that what we are culturally taught clashes with self-care. The collectivist nature of Asian cultures emphasizes on seeing ourselves as part of a group supporting each other's needs rather than as individuals, and values like sacrifice, selflessness, conflict avoidance, and harmony are prioritized over the needs of the individual.

For instance, regardless of how tired you are after a full day at work, you may have to go to a social gathering in the family because that's what we are taught to do. This adds to fatigue and exhaustion, and perhaps even guilt if you decide not to go.

And that's where boundary setting comes in. It's an important tool/method that enables women leaders to stay in control of their time and energy. As a practice, boundary setting helps you to clearly define and maintain your personal limits and needs across various aspects of life. Setting boundaries help safeguard mental, emotional, and physical health by preventing overcommitment, stress, and burnout. Clear boundaries contribute to healthier, more respectful relationships both personally and professionally.

It's an essential skill for managing work–life balance, personal well-being, and healthy relationships.

Boundary setting involves personal boundaries where we set emotional, physical, or mental rules and limits within relationships and interactions. And then there are professional boundaries which involve limits and rules set around work responsibilities, interactions with colleagues, and work–life balance.

Types of Boundaries

Emotional Boundaries

- Protect your emotional well-being by not taking on others' problems as your own or managing emotional energy.

Time Boundaries

- Allocate your time effectively between work, personal life, and rest. Spend your time on your priorities first rather than on other people's work.

Physical Boundaries

- Value and define your personal space, your need for privacy, and body autonomy especially with things like rest, sleep, alone time, etc.

Intellectual Boundaries

- Respectful dialogue, not dismissal, defines healthy intellectual boundaries. They help you value your own and others' ideas, foster curiosity, learn through open communication, and not shut down diverse perspectives.

Work–life Boundaries

- Delineate between professional responsibilities and personal life to ensure one doesn't overwhelmingly encroach on the other.

Along with the action of defining and drawing your boundaries, it's important to acknowledge and accept that a mindset shift is also required for change. First and foremost is recognizing that setting boundaries is a form of self-respect and is necessary for your health and well-being.

You may need to move away from traditional ways of thinking towards a more sustainable and fulfilling approach to leadership and personal life. Here are some shifts you can begin to make:

Shifting from Pleasing Everyone to Prioritizing Self

- Moving away from the need to meet everyone's expectations. Recognising that saying 'no' is a powerful tool for managing time and priorities.

Moving from Perfection to Good Enough

- Letting go of the idea of being perfect in every role. Embrace the concept that 'good enough' is often sufficient, and perfection is not only unrealistic but also unsustainable.

Viewing Boundaries as Strength, Not Weakness

- Recognizing that setting and enforcing boundaries is a sign of strength and self-awareness. Boundaries are essential for managing energy and commitments effectively.

These mindset shifts are critical for women leaders to find balance, lead effectively, and live more fulfilling lives. They represent a holistic approach to leadership, recognizing the interconnectedness of professional success, personal well-being, and overall life satisfaction. Here are quick steps to setting boundaries:

- Identify what you value and need in different aspects of your life.
- Clearly define what is acceptable and unacceptable for you.
- Assertively communicate these boundaries to others. Don't leave room for misinterpretation in your communication. Be clear and concise about your expectations. For example, 'I'm not available for meetings after 6 p.m.' or 'I prefer to handle this task independently.'
- Consistently uphold your boundaries and remind others when they are being crossed. Some people might initially resist your boundaries. Be prepared to politely but firmly decline requests that violate your limits.
- Be willing to re-evaluate and adjust your boundaries as your life circumstances change.

Lean on supportive friends, family, or professionals who understand the importance of healthy boundaries. Boundary setting is a skill that improves with practice and requires patience both with oneself and others.

The WISE Model

We have covered a lot in the chapter about how to strike the balance that works for you. Finding balance is a skill that becomes easier with practice. To make it easy to remember and practice, we have put together a model that combines the crux of our research—the WISE Model of Balance.

This model is a straightforward yet comprehensive guide for women leaders to achieve a more balanced and fulfilling life through a structured yet adaptable approach to managing the complexities of professional and personal life. Its four components are (*Figure 4*):

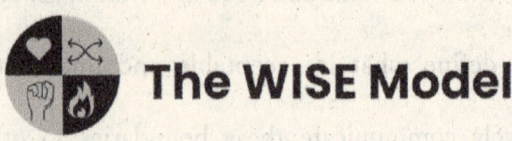

The WISE Model

Well-being (W) 💜
Make your physical, mental, and emotional health a top priority. Incorporate regular exercise into your routine, ensure you get enough sleep. Don't neglect mental health; practise stress reduction techniques like meditation or mindfulness. Regularly engage in activities that nourish your emotional well-being. Whether it's spending time with loved ones, pursuing hobbies, or simply having some quiet time alone.

Integration (I) ✄
Instead of striving for a perfect balance, aim for a balanced integration of your work and personal life. Understand that there will be times when work takes precedence and other times when personal life needs more attention. Advocate for and utilize flexible work arrangements. View your life as a whole where each part, be it work, family, or personal interests, complements and supports the others.

Self-Advocacy (S) ✊
Be clear and assertive in communicating your needs and boundaries to your team, management, and family. It's essential to articulate what you need to succeed and maintain balance. Be comfortable in saying no. Don't shy away from delegating tasks both at work and home. Utilize your support network—professional contacts, family, friends—for assistance and guidance.

Energy (E) 🔥
Focus on activities and habits that boost energy levels and maintain vitality. Cultivate a positive, can-do attitude that fuels resilience and drive. Implement work habits that sustain energy throughout the day, such as taking short breaks, practising time management techniques, and setting realistic goals to prevent burnout.

Figure 4

Remember, achieving balance is a personal and dynamic process. It requires ongoing effort, self-awareness, and the willingness to adapt as circumstances change. By following the WISE model, you're not just working towards balance; you're cultivating a lifestyle that supports your overall well-being, professional success, and personal fulfilment.

No One Way

As with most things there is no one way to find balance. Balance should be defined and approached differently by each person based on a reflection of unique personal values, life circumstances, and priorities. The concept of balance is highly individualized and what works for one leader may not necessarily work for another.

Here's an illustrative comparison between two leaders, Jackie and Linda, to demonstrate how balance can differ:

EXAMPLE A
DESIGNATION

Jackie, chief technology officer: Jackie is in her early forties, married, and a mother of one. As a CTO of a large tech company, her role is demanding and fast-paced.

APPROACH TO BALANCE

- **Early morning routine:** Jackie starts her day early with a mix of exercise and meditation, finding this essential for her focus and energy.
- **Structured workday:** She keeps a very structured schedule at work, maximizing her productivity during office hours so she can leave work at the office.
- **Family evenings:** Jackie dedicates her evenings exclusively to family time, helping with homework, and engaging in family activities.
- **Digital detox:** She practises a digital detox during weekends, disconnecting from work emails and calls to fully engage in personal life and hobbies.

DESIGNATION

Linda, chief technology officer: Linda, also in her early forties, and a mother of two, holds the same position in a competing tech company. She is known for her innovative approach and leadership.

APPROACH TO BALANCE

- **Flexible work hours:** Linda opts for a more flexible work schedule. She sometimes works late evenings but balances this by spending afternoons with her children.
- **Work-from-home days:** She regularly works from home, which allows her to be more present for family responsibilities and reduces commute time.
- **Professional networking:** Linda often integrates socializing with her professional development, attending industry events and dinners.
- **Weekend activities:** She dedicates her weekends to a mix of family outings and personal time, often involving outdoor activities or pursuing her interest in photography.

COMPARISON

- **Daily structure vs. Flexibility:** Jackie maintains a strict separation between work and personal life with a structured daily routine. Linda, on the other hand, prefers a more fluid approach, blending work and family life throughout her day.
- **Technology interaction:** Jackie practices regular digital detoxes, while Linda integrates technology more seamlessly into her personal life.
- **Leisure and family time:** Both prioritize family, but Jackie focuses on daily family evenings, whereas Linda balances work and family throughout the day and reserves weekends for leisure.

CONCLUSION

Jackie and Linda, both CTOs and mothers, demonstrate different strategies for achieving balance. Jackie's approach is more about compartmentalization, creating distinct boundaries between work and personal life. Linda's approach is more integrated, allowing for flexibility and blending different aspects of her life. Their examples highlight that even at the same corporate level and in similar roles, balance can be achieved in various ways, tailored to individual preferences, family needs, and personal styles.

EXAMPLE B

Let's consider another example of two women leaders, each with distinct lifestyles and priorities, to illustrate how their approaches to achieving balance can differ.

DESIGNATION

Simran, tech startup founder: Simran is in her early thirties, single, and the founder of a rapidly growing tech startup.

DEFINITION OF BALANCE

For Simran, balance means managing her high-demand career while maintaining an active social life and personal development.

APPROACH TO BALANCE

- **Work intensity:** She often works long hours during weekdays, driven by her passion for her startup.

- **Social and networking events:** Weekends are reserved for socializing and attending industry networking events, which she enjoys and uses to promote her business.
- **Personal growth:** Simran dedicates time for personal hobbies like reading and attending professional development courses, often late in the evenings.
- **Health routine:** Regular yoga sessions and a strict diet keep her energized and focused.

DESIGNATION

Mina, non-profit organization director: Mina, in her late forties, is a mother of two teenagers and leads a large non-profit organization.

DEFINITION OF BALANCE

Mina's balance is about meaningful contribution to her work while being actively involved in her children's lives.

APPROACH TO BALANCE

- **Family time:** Mina prioritizes her mornings and evenings for family activities, ensuring she's present for breakfast and dinner with her children.
- **Work scheduling:** Her workday is strictly scheduled, focusing on impactful activities and delegation to her team to manage the non-profit efficiently.
- **Community involvement:** Weekends are often spent in community service activities with her family, aligning her personal values with family bonding.
- **Self-care:** Mina ensures regular self-care routines, including walking and meditation, to maintain her mental and physical health.

COMPARISON

- **Life stage & priorities:** Simran's approach is shaped by her life stage and single status, focusing on career growth and social networking. Mina, however, balances her established career with her role as a mother, emphasizing family involvement and community service.
- **Time management:** Simran's schedule is more fluid, blending personal development with her professional role. Mina, on the other hand, adheres to a more structured schedule to ensure she meets both her family and professional commitments.
- **Focus on health:** While both prioritize health, their methods differ. Simran focuses on high-energy activities like yoga, while Mina prefers more calming practices like walking and meditation.

CONCLUSION

These examples of Simran and Mina demonstrate that balance is highly personal and varies significantly based on individual circumstances, priorities, and life stages. Both are successful leaders but approach balance in ways that best suit their personal lives and career demands. Their stories highlight that there is no singular way to achieve balance; it's about finding what works best for each individual.

SUMMARY

Importance of balance: Balance isn't just desirable, it's crucial for a healthy, fulfilling life. It's about finding the right equilibrium between different areas to achieve personal and professional growth while maintaining your well-being.

Boundary setting: This is a crucial skill for women leaders to thrive in demanding roles while prioritizing their overall well-being. Setting boundaries is an ongoing process of self-awareness, communication, and self-respect. Take control of your time, energy, and well-being.

WISE Model: This model emphasizes a holistic approach to work-life balance, prioritizing your well-being, integrating different aspects of your life, advocating for yourself, and managing your energy wisely.

Well-being (W): Prioritize physical, mental, and emotional health through activities like exercise, sleep, stress management, and self-care.

Integration (I): Instead of strict separation, aim for a blended integration of work and personal life, acknowledging their interconnectedness and adapting priorities as needed. Utilize flexible work arrangements when possible.

Self-Advocacy (S): Communicate your needs and boundaries clearly to others, both at work and personally. Don't be afraid to say no, delegate tasks, and advocate for what allows you to thrive.

Energy (E): Manage your energy like a resource. Implement practices like time management, breaks, and realistic goals to avoid burnout. Replenish your energy through activities that boost vitality and maintain a positive attitude.

REFLECT: SELF-ASSESS: ACTION

Reflect what we just discussed in the chapter above and use the following four blockers to **self-assess** where you are on the balance journey and write out one **action** that you can take to build your balance.

Sustain	Shrink
What behaviours should you continue to practice? Positive behaviours that are working well for you. For example, taking regular breaks from work for physical well-being like going on walks, exercising, etc.	What behaviours are not serving you well in your career? Habits that you want to see less of. For example, saying yes to doing everything yourself instead of delegating or reprioritizing.
The behaviours I want to sustain are . . . _____ _____ _____ _____	The behaviours I want to shrink are . . . _____ _____ _____ _____

Discard	Amplify
What is not working well for you?	What behaviours that you currently demonstrate need to be practised more?
Getting rid of behaviours that aren't working for you at all.	Practices that you should do more of.
For example, not sleeping enough or skipping meals.	For example, making time for personal pursuits and hobbies.
The behaviours I want to discard are . . .	The behaviours I want to amplify are . . .
_____	_____
_____	_____
_____	_____
_____	_____

Take Action

- What is your one practice that you will put into action to achieve balance?

5

The Defining Success Rule

When we started working on the outline of our book, we assumed that women would define success in terms of promotions, scope, and power. However, when we started interviewing various women leaders and asked them how they define success, what we heard surprised us. Here are some quotes from our speakers:

'Success encompasses financial viability of one's business as well as enriching relationships—with employees who view their work as a calling, with clients who trust you to meet their evolving needs year after year, and most importantly, with family through shared memories, laughter and togetherness.'

'Success for me is to reach inner peace.'

'Success is defined in the day-to-day, based on who you strive to become and the priorities you set. Ultimately it involves making micro choices and trade-offs aligned to your values that compound into a wider, lasting impact.'

'I think success for me is how you learn from failures, which is really important.'

'For me success is really about how you recover and can redefine yourself, and put yourself on that growth trajectory, at work or in life.'

More and more women were including impact, family, spiritual growth, and personal learning when talking about success. They were expanding its definition beyond just achieving milestones and goals in a corporate setting. That's when we realized that when we write about 'success' we must present its expansive meaning rather than leaning on its narrow, traditional definition. In fact, we realized that when we both also shared what professional success means to us, it reflected what we heard from our speakers—learning something new every day, making an impact, and contributing to the growth and success of others in the organization.

Our conviction that women leaders today are looking at success more holistically grew and led us to move away from writing just about success to write about growth.

Growth and Success

Growth and success are related concepts. They can occur independently and together. They differ in their focus, nature, and how they manifest themselves. Growth can lead to success, as personal and professional development often results in achieving desired goals. Conversely, pursuing success can spur growth, as the challenges encountered along the way foster learning and development.

For instance, success is typically defined by the achievement of specific goals or objectives like a promotion in the organization. Whereas, growth is more about the journey, the process of learning or developing, focusing on the progression over time like when you are learning the nuances of people management on the job.

Next, success often involves external recognition or validation, such as awards, promotions, financial gains, or public acknowledgment, like when you complete a training programme successfully to gain the intended knowledge and skills to get a certification. Success is often quantifiable, measured against predefined criteria or benchmarks, like income levels, job titles, or accomplishments. On the other hand, growth involves personal development, learning, and self-improvement, acquiring new skills, expanding knowledge, and evolving attitudes and behaviours. Growth is usually measured qualitatively and is about the depth and richness of experiences and learning. Overcoming a fear of public speaking is one such example of growth.

What constitutes 'success' can vary greatly from person to person and is often tied to personal values or a goal someone sets for themselves. For some, it might be achieving financial stability and owning a home, while for others, it might be travelling the world and having enriching experiences. Growth, however, is a lifelong journey, not a destination. It's about constantly learning, developing new skills, and expanding your knowledge base. There's always room for improvement, regardless of age or experience. Consider someone passionate about fitness. Even after achieving a fitness goal like running a marathon, growth would involve continued training, learning new exercises, and pushing oneself further. The journey to becoming a better runner never truly ends.

For all leaders, differentiating between growth and success is essential. Balancing the pursuit of success with a commitment to ongoing growth is the key to sustainable and fulfilling leadership and life.

While success and growth are deeply connected, this book focuses primarily on the concept of growth, and our main goal is to help you develop and reach your full potential.

Traditional Approach to Success

Traditionally the focus in corporate settings has been on success especially in the context of leadership and career achievement. The following are a typical set of universal and tangible indicators:

Financial Achievement

- Traditionally, a high income, lucrative bonuses, and substantial wealth accumulation are primary indicators of success.

Professional Advancement

- Climbing the corporate ladder to reach high-ranking positions such as CEO, director, or manager is often seen as a hallmark of success. Holding a position of power and authority in an organization is highly valued.

Recognition and Awards

- Receiving accolades, awards, and public recognition for professional accomplishments is another traditional marker of success. This includes industry awards, company acknowledgments, and public honours.

Influence and Power

- The ability to influence decisions, policies, and people is often equated with success. This includes having a strong professional network and being a key decision-maker.

Productivity and Achievements

- Measuring success by the number of projects completed, deals closed, or innovations introduced is common. This approach focuses on quantifiable outputs and achievements.

Educational Attainment

- High levels of formal education, such as obtaining advanced degrees from prestigious institutions, are traditionally seen as indicators of success.

While these traditional metrics of success are still relevant and valued, there's a growing recognition of the need for a more holistic, inclusive, and personalized definition of success.

Growth and Maslow's Hierarchy

In the early stages of her journey, Uma's focus was solely on basic needs. Her first job wasn't about fancy titles or high salaries; it was simply about securing a stable living situation, even if it meant sharing a cramped apartment with four roommates. Once that need was fulfilled, a new one arose; the need for financial security, the need to have her own home. It seemed as if the goalposts of her aspirations kept shifting with each achieved basic need.

Today, her sense of success revolves around the micro-moments. For example, the heartfelt messages received on her recent birthday, especially the cards from her nephews detailing the positive impact she's had on their lives. These, she has come to realize, are the true moments of arrival. They are small, unexpected, and brimming with genuine connection. While they might seem insignificant in the grand scheme of things, they hold the most meaning for her now.

Uma recalled that when she was younger her definition of success was interesting. She vividly recalled a Lexus car advertisement featuring someone driving a different Lexus each day. This sparked a childhood dream—having a driveway filled with seven Lexus and the ability to buy anything in a store without a glance at the price tag. And yes, she eventually achieved that dream. However, it began with addressing her basic needs and gradually climbing the ladder of success.

This is the story of Uma Thana Balasingam, the founder and CEO of the Lean In Network, Singapore, and ELEVATE. With over twenty years of technology sales leadership across Asia Pacific and Japan, her work is currently focused on empowering girls and advancing women in the workplace. Uma's story highlights how her definition of growth evolved as she grew in her career.

↔

Our conversation with other women leaders, too, showed this interesting pattern when it came to the definition of success. Almost all of them said that when they started off their careers the definition of success was about the promotion, salary increment, and titles. As they moved up the ladder the definition evolved to being fully engaged at work, doing meaningful work, and making an impact.

As we reflected more on this pattern, we saw that this aligned well with Maslow's hierarchy of needs. Maslow's hierarchy of needs is a theory in psychology that suggests there are five basic needs that motivate human behaviour. These needs are arranged in a pyramid, with the most basic needs at the bottom and the more complex needs at the top. According to the theory, we need to fulfil each level of needs before we can move on to the next level.

Ladder of Growth

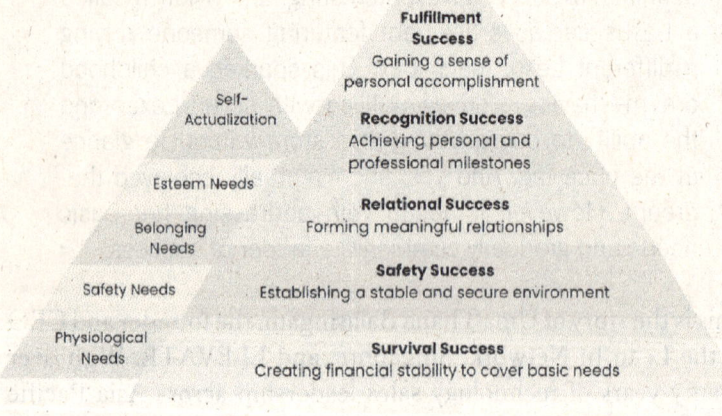

Figure 5a

Here is how we are attempting to draw the connections between different levels of Maslow's hierarchy and the changing definitions of success i.e. the 'Ladder of Growth' (*Figure 5a*). This ladder illustrates that growth is not static but evolves as individuals grow and their needs change. It highlights the importance of recognizing and valuing different aspects of success at various stages of life and personal development.

1. **Physiological Needs—Survival Success:** Achieving financial stability to cover basic needs like food, shelter, and basic living conditions is the initial measure of success.
2. **Safety Needs—Security Success:** Here, establishing a stable and secure environment for oneself and one's family, financial security, health, and well-being measure success.
3. **Love and Belonging Needs—Relational Success:** Success here is about forming meaningful relationships, being part of a community, and having a sense of belonging.
4. **Esteem Needs—Recognition Success:** Success in this context is about achieving personal and professional milestones that garner respect and admiration from others.
5. **Self-Actualization—Fulfilment Success:** Success is defined by pursuing passions, engaging in activities that are deeply fulfilling, and gaining a sense of personal accomplishment.

As individuals progress through these levels, the definition of success evolves from external and material achievements to more internal contentment and personal fulfilment.

Challenging Traditional Definition of Success

The traditional definitions of success often work against women in several ways, particularly in leadership roles. In order to achieve traditional success, especially in the traditionally male-dominated sphere of business, women may feel the need to display traits historically associated with male leaders, such as aggression, competitiveness, and assertiveness. In our earlier chapter on visibility, we saw that women who display these traits might be perceived negatively while those who do not demonstrate these behaviours are seen as less successful.

The traditional metrics often overlook skills such as empathy, self-awareness, and emotional intelligence which are crucial for building strong teams, resolving conflicts, and creating positive work environments. The capacity to navigate challenges, adapt to change, and bounce back from setbacks is crucial for long-term success, and this resilience that is often an unseen process is not always acknowledged as a key component of success. A broader definition allows for recognition of leadership qualities like empathy, collaboration, and emotional intelligence, which are often strong suits of women leaders.

Many of these traits are developed through experience and practices requiring a lot of time and introspection, and not necessarily through attending a course or training. A more holistic view of success encourages continuous learning and adaptation, which is crucial for long-term career growth. This is particularly beneficial for women leaders who face evolving challenges and opportunities in their careers.

Traditionally, success often prioritizes career accomplishments at the expense of personal well-being. Broadening the definition of success to include contributions to society and community resonates with many women leaders who strive to create positive changes beyond their organizations. This aligns with the growing emphasis on corporate social responsibility and ethical leadership. A more inclusive definition of success acknowledges the importance of this balance, valuing contributions both inside and outside the workplace.

Women's career trajectories can be non-linear, with breaks or shifts due to various life stages or personal choices like taking a break for pursuing education or taking parental leave. Broadening the definition of success accommodates these varied paths, recognizing that career breaks or transitions do not diminish a leader's capability or potential.

Cultural views on gender roles significantly affect how success is defined for women. Often women's achievements might be seen primarily through the lens of their roles as mothers and wives. Another example can be how in some cultures long working hours and assertive leadership styles are valued, which can disadvantage women who may adopt different work styles or require flexible schedules due to family commitments. Understanding these cultural nuances is crucial, especially for global organizations and for women leaders who navigate diverse cultural environments.

The emphasis on constant availability and long working hours as indicators of commitment to success can be particularly challenging for women who often shoulder a disproportionate share of family and caregiving responsibilities. In Asian cultures, societal expectations about gender roles can limit women's career choices and their aspirations for success. For instance, in some Asian cultures, women may be discouraged from travelling or taking overseas assignments in order to prioritize family commitments.

In essence, a broader definition of success is not just about rethinking achievement. It's about creating an environment where women leaders can thrive, are encouraged to pursue continuous growth, and are recognized for their unique contributions, styles, and values. It is also about recognizing the impact that society and culture have on the success of women. This approach paves the way for a more equitable, dynamic, and sustainable leadership landscape which challenges stereotypes and biases.

Success Trap

Ever felt like your worth is measured by your latest achievement or how much applause you get?

When was the last time you did something just because you loved it, not because it looked good on your resume?

Do you feel you are running on a treadmill that's always speeding up?

Have you caught yourself eyeing a colleague's achievements and feeling a bit green?

Do you know where you really want to go in the long haul?

One of the pitfalls of running after external markers of success is the phenomenon known as success trap. Speaking to women leaders as part of the research for the book this phrase came up commonly, especially in women who were in the early and mid-part of their careers.

Success trap is a situation where an individual becomes overly focused on achieving traditional markers of success, such as high-ranking positions, financial gains, prestigious awards, or public recognition, often at the expense of personal fulfilment, values, or long-term well-being.

Luckily, there are some tell-tale signs that can tell you if you are getting trapped. Recognizing them can help you overcome the downsides of being caught in a success trap.

One of the first signs of being in the success trap is when you begin to overemphasize external validation and approval for your work. You begin to associate success by what is recognized and applauded by others such as promotions, accolades, or social status.

Next, when you are in the success trap, you begin to neglect your personal values and fulfilment. All aspects of life that provide intrinsic satisfaction are often side-lined in pursuit of external success markers. The continuous chase for the next achievement leads to burnout, stress, and a lack of work–life balance. It feels like a never-ending cycle that may not lead to genuine contentment.

The success trap can foster a mindset where success is viewed in comparative terms, leading to constant comparison with others' achievements. You begin to feel 'trapped' on gaining short-term achievements and quick wins rather than long-term goals and sustainable growth. This short-sighted approach can hinder personal and professional development.

Success trap often involves a deep-seated fear of failure or of falling behind peers. This fear can stifle creativity, risk-taking, and the pursuit of unconventional paths that might lead to more meaningful achievements. It can make us so scared of failing or losing ground that we stop taking risks or trying new things.

For women leaders, the success trap can be particularly challenging. They may feel pressure to conform to traditional success standards in professional environments while balancing societal and personal expectations. An example could be the expectation to constantly be available and put in long hours, regardless of personal commitments. This can be particularly challenging for women navigating childcare or eldercare responsibilities.

Escaping the success trap involves redefining success on more personal and holistic terms, aligning professional goals with personal values, and embracing a more balanced approach to life and work.

↔

Ritu's story below showcases how she too was caught in the success trap in her corporate journey. It wasn't until she was forty that she started to design her own growth journey.

Ritu's Story

I considered myself a high-achieving executive having started my career as a Financial Analyst in Gillette and quickly moving to becoming a Vice President in GE Capital. I was driven by traditional markers of success, I had climbed the corporate ladder quickly, I was travelling the world on business assignments, and had worked abroad in three countries. By my mid-thirties, I held a senior executive position, earning a high salary and commanding respect in my field. My sense of worth was closely linked to my professional achievements and external recognition. My identity was deeply entwined with my job title.

I worked long hours and sacrificed weekends for professional goals. Constant comparison with peers and a fear of being perceived as less successful drove me to take on unsustainable workloads and responsibilities.

Ironically, at the same time, this led me to take less risks, and my learning curve became flat and plateaued. I didn't invest time in learning anything new and I didn't focus on upskilling. I was focused on the short term instead of the long term.

Luckily for me, it was that time that my manager got his team to work with a coach. It was during this coaching journey that I started to gain clarity, and that led me to decide my future course and define my own path to success, or rather, growth.

That coaching experience gave me a taste of the impact of coaching and became a catalyst for me to start my own journey of becoming a coach few years later.

Having said that, from time to time, I still find myself getting drawn to the success trap where I am comparing myself to other consultants or looking for validation on social media. But recognizing the tell-tale signs of the success trap helps!

I know I'm not alone in this. For my first book, *Leader's Block* I had spoken to more than 200 leaders and every one of them had experienced some version of this. The key is to recognize it, acknowledge it, and then take action to come out of it.

So, now when I find myself getting restless thinking that I am not doing enough or I'm constantly monitoring the engagement on my LinkedIn posts, I quickly check myself, and remind myself of the bigger goal that I am pursuing.

↔

Rewriting What Success Means to You

To address the discrete natures of success and growth, it's important to rewrite success in more inclusive and flexible terms. We want to showcase the broader perspective of women leaders we spoke to who have redefined success on their own terms.

The wisdom they garnered from their experience can help us bring unique perspectives and strengths to leadership roles.

Defining your own success can be empowering. Your own definition of success ensures that your goals and aspirations align with your personal values, beliefs, and life circumstances. This alignment fosters a sense of authenticity, allowing you to pursue goals that truly resonate with you, rather than following externally imposed standards. Defining success for yourself means taking control of your life and career, making proactive decisions, and feeling confident in your path.

When you define success in your terms, you're more likely to be motivated and engaged in your pursuits. You're working towards goals that have personal significance, which can drive passion and commitment. You can include aspects of well-being and life satisfaction, not just professional achievements. This broader view can lead to a more balanced and fulfilling life, where success is not just about work but also about personal growth, relationships, and happiness. You end up defining success that's unique and meaningful to you.

This sense of empowerment is particularly important for women, who may face societal and professional barriers. Personalized success definitions can adapt as you grow and as your life circumstances change. This flexibility is crucial in a dynamic world where professional and personal landscapes are constantly evolving.

↔

This glimpse of our conversation with Arpita Pal Agrawal—MD & CEO of Dia Vikas Capital, India—on how she rewrote the rules of success illustrates how she defined what success meant for her, took the steps to keep learning, and lived by her mantra to 'never settle'. Arpita grew up in India, and has since been working in various multinational companies and most recently has been leading Dia Vikas Capital (subsidiary of Opportunity International), an impact investor that funds Indian social impact institutions.

From a young age, I've always been driven by a need to understand the bigger picture. Early in my career, I worked as a software engineer abroad, but I felt disconnected from the company's goals. My contributions seemed like isolated tasks. This yearning for context led me to pursue an MBA, giving me a broader understanding of the larger business and commercial landscape.

Even after consulting across diverse industries, gaining new skills and conquering each challenge, a sense of stagnation crept in. My internal barometer has always been this: when I start dragging myself to work and dread getting up in the morning, it's time for a change. I'm not suggesting everyone quit their jobs impulsively, but it's a sign that your current role might not be stimulating enough for you. Seeking a deeper purpose and wanting to give back in a way closer to how I knew best, I embarked on a new adventure—impact investing—when I was nearing fifty.

My personal growth journey thrives on expanding my perspectives and mastering unfamiliar domains that align with my values, like governance, sustainability, and inclusion for the disadvantaged. While initial transitions are often challenging and met with scepticism, I believe embracing this unsettledness is key to avoiding complacency.

Finding what ignites you requires stepping outside your comfort zone. I've transitioned careers multiple times, each requiring dedicated learning. Even when preparing for board roles, despite my experience, I went to Harvard Business School to gain a formal framework. I believe continuous learning and pushing my boundaries are essential for growth.

So, while I advocate against settling, it's crucial to be comfortable with discomfort. Stepping outside your comfort zone allows you to gain a larger perspective, explore new possibilities and ultimately, define your own unique path.

↔

Even though it sounds obvious, when we run leadership programmes for women leaders we often find that women are reluctant to define their own success due to a combination of societal, cultural, and psychological factors. Do I lean in or lean out, scale up or scale back, put my hand up or wait for the right time?

Uncertainty can be unnerving, but we want to say that don't give up your agency. You have a choice to design the path that works for you.

REWRITE THE RULES

The first rule of success that needs to be rewritten is that it needs to include growth which encompasses various aspects of life contributing to a holistic sense of achievement and fulfilment.

The landscape of success is evolving. Here are a few powerful ways to redefine your own success and make a meaningful impact in a changing world. These are based on what the women leaders we interviewed have rewritten and practise:

Pursue Meaningful Scope, Not Just Titles

Promotions are not the only indicators of success. Seek out opportunities to expand your responsibilities by volunteering for challenging projects, proposing process improvements in the work you do, or take the initiative to lead smaller pieces of work within your existing role. Your proactive contributions can demonstrate your value. Make sure to focus on the impact you can make, not just your title. Building a reputation for excellence in a specific domain holds more weight than seeking a higher position.

↔

Patricia Feria Lim is the vice president of operations at Thinking Machines Data Science, a data and AI tech consultancy that operates in Singapore, the Philippines, and Thailand. She has worked in finance, operations, and social impact in the US and Southeast Asia. She shared with us her philosophy for pursuing career growth.

A few months into my first sabbatical, I chanced upon this incredible story of a creative executive in New York who shuts down his company every seven years to take a year-long sabbatical and load up on ideas and inspiration for what could be next. It blew my mind! His story challenged traditional thinking about constantly chasing the next deal or promotion, and waiting until retirement to explore possibilities, and personal interests. By then, one might not have the same energy or health.

He proposed an alternative: intersperse these 'pauses' throughout your career! 'Why wait?' he said.

I felt validated! I had just taken my first leap of faith (moving from New York to the Philippines) and here I am now, three different careers and two 'purposeful pauses' later.

I recognize what I've done is a privilege and not everyone might be comfortable defying the traditional logic of—apply, interview, get the offer, and then resign. However, my philosophy is grounded in three core principles that have guided my life and career choices to date: meaningful learning, relationships, and purpose.

I think of these principles as the legs of a stool. When even one leg is missing, the entire stool (me!) becomes wobbly. Throughout my career, I've always strived to ensure all three legs are present. The sabbaticals or 'purposeful pauses' I've taken have helped open new opportunities and create the balanced and fulfilling life I have and love.

↔

Invest In Yourself

Don't just maintain your current skill set. Instead, stay ahead of the curve by actively acquiring new skills and expertise relevant to your field. This will require making time in your busy schedule however you can and weave learning into your schedule by utilizing online courses and certifications, or attending workshops organized by your workplace that aim to expand your knowledge and enhance your skill set beyond your job requirements. This will also showcase your commitment to continuous learning and growth, making you a valuable asset to any team.

↔

Pratima Amonkar is one of the women leaders we interviewed, and she told us about how she has invested in keeping her knowledge relevant. She is Microsoft's ASEAN Lead for Business Strategy. She has been on the forefront, driving the digital transformation of businesses and lives through the power of the cloud and comes with a rich experience of twenty years in leadership roles within the tech industry. She hails from India and is currently based in Singapore.

In a fast-paced field like tech, staying ahead requires continuous learning. While juggling schedules can be tricky, I've found a mix of formal and informal approaches work best for me.

I leverage audiobooks, podcasts, and summaries for on-the-go learning, while my organization's learning culture supports a structured development plan. This plan involves identifying gaps between my current skills and desired career goals, then filling them through targeted training.

Formal options like internal programmes and online platforms like LinkedIn Learning provide a strong foundation, while on-the-job projects in new areas like AI or cloud computing offer valuable hands-on experience and networking opportunities. I recently took an MIT course on AI, gaining valuable knowledge and connecting with a global cohort. While informal learning is important, I believe in the power of structured training to build a strong foundation for further exploration. I used to avoid formal training, but I've come to realize its value, especially in tech.

This multi-pronged approach, coupled with a growth mindset, has been instrumental in my professional and personal growth.

↔

Build Your Network and Community

- While at work, don't just connect with colleagues within your immediate circle. Find the time to expand your network by attending industry events, participating in online forums, or connecting with professionals on social media. Building genuine relationships with others in your field opens doors to new opportunities, collaborations, and recognition.

- Look for opportunities to work with others on external projects or initiatives outside your organization like community service, volunteering, and being part of executive committees. These collaborations can not only enhance your skills and knowledge but also expand your reach and impact beyond your immediate role.

- Find ways to share your knowledge with others through contributing to blogs or publications, presenting your findings at conferences, and mentoring others to share your expertise with colleagues. This helps in building your reputation as a thought leader.

In doing all this, don't let work consume your life and be sure to spend time nurturing relationships with friends and family.

Their support provides perspective and boosts your well-being, essential for career growth.

↔

Going back to Patricia's career journey again, she shared with us how her career path wasn't forged through formal networking events, but through the power of informal connections and the meaningful relationships she's built and nurtured over the years.

My career highlights the unexpected power of genuine connections.

First, shifting from sell side to the buy side in Finance was not driven or motivated by a headhunter or recruiter. Rather, in a community of Asian leaders, I had a meaningful conversation with an individual who eventually hired me into his team at a hedge fund.

A few years later, moving back to the Philippines, I wouldn't have discovered Teach for the Philippines if not for a chance encounter with my sister's classmate, Evan, who I looked out for while he was at UPenn.

I wasn't thinking about securing future favours; my genuine care stemmed from an earnest desire to connect with my sister's friends. Our friendship opened a door to a most fulfilling experience. Evan was instrumental in connecting me with the founders of Teach for the Philippines when I first moved back from the US.

Similarly, seven years later, after retiring from Teach for the Philippines, my informal network came alive again. A friend I supported through coaching recognized my unique blend of experiences in professional services (in finance) and operations (in a startup-stage nonprofit) and connected me with a startup founder who was seeking those exact qualifications.

These have instilled in me a deep appreciation for the power of authentic connections, reminding me that sometimes, unexpected encounters can lead to the most significant opportunities for growth.

My commitment now is to pay forward these very gifts to others who are looking to explore or are unclear about their future careers. It's been most fulfilling to create deeper connections and expand my 'village' through this process.

↔

Challenge Yourself

Develop new hobbies or pick up your old ones where you left them. Explore activities like that resonate with you and you'll find that you build resilience, adaptability, and problem-solving skills applicable to your career. Volunteer and contribute your time and skills to local charities. Develop empathy, communication, and leadership skills while making a positive impact. Try something new, push yourself, challenge yourself, and while you may experience setbacks, learn from your failures rather than giving up.

↔

Aarti Dabas spoke to us about her relationship with success and growth when it came to her career. Aarti is the chief media officer at Formula E Holdings. She is currently based in UAE and is a senior leader within the sports industry with over twenty years of experience in delivering strategies to drive sustainable growth, engage diverse fans, and increase revenues.

Success isn't a one-size-fits-all definition. When you talk about overachieving, I still feel like I haven't accomplished enough. People tell me to be kinder to myself, and I realize they're right. Women especially need to acknowledge their achievements—we're often too hard on ourselves.

For me, true success lies in learning from failures. Three years ago, I was asked to move on from a job I'd been at for twelve years. It was a defining moment, not because of some argument, but because of the leader's behaviour. It made me think—how can I turn challenges into opportunities?

Success is about how you recover and redefine yourself after a setback. Who I am today is the sum of all my experiences, good and bad, from my family background to everything else life has thrown my way.

Bouncing back, learning from mistakes, and letting go—that's what defines success for me. Working in sports, I've seen the power of self-belief in both male and female athletes. It's crucial. Believe in yourself, in your abilities, and don't let anyone dim your light.

Self-belief is something women often struggle with more than men. But hard work is just as important. The harder you work, the luckier you get. There's no replacement for sheer effort. The key is to deliver and prove yourself.

So, believe in yourself, work hard, and focus on your learnings. Life has its hiccups, but don't dwell on blame or excuses. Be empathetic but keep pushing forward. That's the path to true success.

↔

Prioritize Well-Being

As discussed in the chapter on achieving balance, focus on physical health, regular exercise, healthy diet, energy, and overall well-being impacts your career performance. Nurture your mental and emotional health by practising mindfulness, seeking professional help if needed, and prioritizing stress management for optimal mental clarity and resilience. Manage your finances by developing a budget and savings plan to reduce stress and create financial security, crucial for career stability.

↔

Rajita's Story

As the uncertainty of 2020 was gripping the world, I wasn't a stranger to it either, both personally and professionally.

During a work meeting, a call from my doctor's office sent shivers down my spine. The EKG from my annual checkup, they said, indicated a possible heart attack, and they urged me to see a specialist.

My day continued with meetings back-to-back, but as evening settled (10.30 p.m. to be precise), the news fully hit me. It didn't make sense. I was a regular yoga practitioner, mindful of my diet, and even carved time for hobbies. A whirlwind of tests and tears later, the verdict arrived: the abnormal EKG was not my heart, it was stress.

This for a seemingly healthy person was a wake-up call. I dove into stress management strategies, learning to disconnect from work, set boundaries, and prioritize breaks. Today, my self-awareness about stress is razor-sharp. I recognize the patterns like poor sleep and headaches, and address them head-on before they snowball by taking breaks, short vacations, and disconnecting from technology.

This heightened awareness hasn't just benefited me personally, it's transformed me into a better leader. By recognizing the signs of stress in myself, I've become more attuned to the same signs in my team. It may sound like a cliché, but self-care truly is the foundation for effective leadership. By prioritizing my own well-being, I'm better equipped to lead with empathy, understanding, and a clear head, ultimately creating a more positive and productive work environment for everyone.

↔

These dimensions are not exhaustive but provide a comprehensive view of what growth can entail. It's important to note that growth is highly individualized, and its definition can vary greatly from one person to another. For women leaders, it often involves navigating these dimensions while balancing unique personal and professional challenges.

By taking charge of your growth, you can carve your own path to success, regardless of traditional markers.

Momentum Map

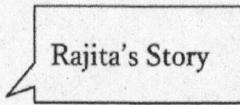

Rajita's Story

A couple of years ago, I began thinking about what the next season of my career would be like. I started to make a list of what I knew it should include. I knew that being an extrovert whatever I plan to do next must involve working closely with a community of like-minded people.

I reflected on what skills I had, what parts of my work and hobbies were most meaningful to me and brought me joy, what my strengths were, and eventually how I could create conditions that allowed me to combine all of those, and yet feel gainfully employed.

I then put what I learned from that reflection exercise together and began planning what I needed to do in a chronological order. That way, by the time I was ready to make a shift in my career, my financial position and my skills and knowledge would be stronger than before. This planning helped me feel in control of my future. Today, I coach many people to create their own plans to move towards the next chapters in their career, and I'd like to share that approach with you.

↔

Introducing the Momentum Map (*Figure 5b*) your personalized plan to propel you towards professional and personal growth in a timeframe that works for you. Forget stagnant and standard goals, Momentum Map is all about consistent action that helps you accelerate your progress towards your growth goals.

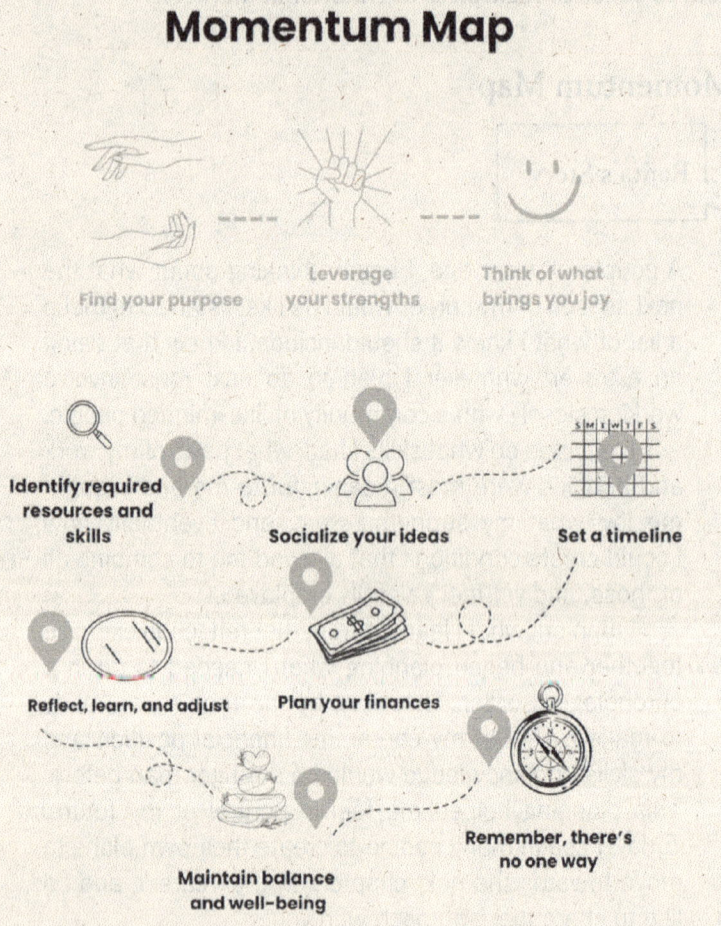

Momentum Map

Find your purpose

Leverage your strengths

Think of what brings you joy

Identify required resources and skills

Socialize your ideas

Set a timeline

Reflect, learn, and adjust

Plan your finances

Maintain balance and well-being

Remember, there's no one way

Figure 5b

Here are some core steps that we recommend you take to create your own Momentum Map:

Think of what brings you joy

- These are areas that bring positive energy and enthusiasm to your work. They are closely aligned with what you value. For instance, volunteering for causes that you believe in like working with an NGO or charity. Understanding your core values can help you align your actions with what truly satisfies you.

Leverage your strengths

- These are areas that you are good at like writing, consulting, project management, or any other areas that you've worked on in your career until now. These could also be a practice you have outside of your day job like yoga, music, painting, or other hobbies that you pursue.
- Focus on your strengths and how they can be utilized to achieve your goals. Understanding and leveraging what you excel at can make your journey more efficient and effective.

Find your purpose

- Once you've given the above two points some thought, you can start identifying what jobs or careers fall in the intersection of your skills and knowledge, and alignment with your values. For instance, for someone it can look like combining their skills of coaching with the desire to help others find clarity in their life journey and become a life coach.

Identify required resources and skills

- Determine what resources (such as time, money, or technology) and skills (like leadership, communication, or technical expertise) you need to achieve your goals.

This could involve pursuing further education, training, or seeking mentorship.

Socialize your ideas

- Speak to people who have taken similar paths as you plan to. There is a lot you can learn from their journeys, both what to do and what not to do. This is where the loose connections that we spoke about in networking become useful. For instance, you could socialize your ideas with friends and they in turn can connect you with people who they know have taken a similar journey.

- Build a supportive network by connecting with mentors who have paved their own impactful paths. Their guidance can provide invaluable insights and encouragement. Build a network of peers and collaborators who share your vision for impact. Collaborative efforts can amplify results and provide diverse perspectives.

Set a timeline

- This is an important step, and it is very personal to you as it depends on your individual life circumstances, obligations, and responsibilities. A word of caution here is knowing that sometimes even the best laid plans may need to shift, and therefore, be flexible and allow for flexibility should that happen. However, view these setbacks and challenges as opportunities for growth. Resilience is key to navigating the ups and downs of any journey. Be open to new ideas and approaches. The ability to innovate and adapt is essential for creating lasting impact.

Plan your finances

- This is a critical aspect especially for women because in most Asian cultures, financial decisions are still made by the men in the house. So, pay a lot of attention to how you will support yourself financially. Focus not just on savings but how to invest it further so that it grows faster. Get a financial planner to help you plan your fiscal goals.

Reflect, learn, and adjust

- Take time to reflect on your progress towards your impactful objectives. Assess what's working, what's not, and why. Based on your reflections, be prepared to make adjustments to your strategies, goals, or methods to better align with your vision for impact. As you evolve, so too will your definition of impact. Revisit and adjust your goals as necessary to align with your current aspirations and the lessons you've learned.
- Documenting your journey can provide insights into your growth and the impact you've made. It can also serve as a roadmap for others. Sharing your experiences, challenges, and successes can inspire and guide others who are embarking on their own quests for impact.

Invest in continuous learning

- Focus on learning, building skills that you'll need for the next season of your career. Embrace a mindset of continuous learning. Seek out resources, courses, and other learning opportunities to gain new skills and knowledge relevant to your goals. Look for interdisciplinary areas that complement your main focus.

Maintain balance and well-being

- This journey is meant to provide joy and fulfilment, and not induce stress, so, pursue your goals in a way that maintains a healthy balance between your professional and personal life. Ensuring your well-being is critical to sustaining your efforts over the long term.

Crafting your Momentum Map empowers you to take control of your career journey. By leveraging your strengths and passions, you can identify a fulfilling path that aligns with your values. Remember, this is a dynamic process. Be open to learning, adapting, and celebrating your progress as you navigate towards creating lasting impact. Share your experiences and inspire others to embark on their own journeys of purpose.

No One Way

Like most things, one thing is clear: there is no one way to follow the path of growth. Depending on the career, life stage, or circumstances, two women could have different paths. Which rung of the Ladder of Growth they are on or how they plan their Momentum Map can differ.

↔

Let's explore the growth journeys of two women leaders, Maya and Zoe, focusing on how their paths to leadership and success evolve over time, highlighting the importance of adaptability, learning, and resilience in their growth.

Maya: The Evolving Entrepreneur

EARLY STAGE

- Maya starts her career as a software developer with a keen interest in educational technology. Her initial success comes from developing an innovative learning app for children. At this stage, Maya's growth is technical skill enhancement and understanding market needs.

MID STAGE

- With her app gaining traction, Maya decides to start her own company focusing on educational technology. She learns the ropes of entrepreneurship, from fundraising to marketing. Maya's growth now includes business management skills, leadership, and strategic thinking. She attends business workshops, seeks mentorship, and joins a network of tech entrepreneurs.

LATER STAGE

- Several years into her journey, Maya's company is a leader in educational technology. She then shifts her focus to global education inequality. Maya's growth transitions to social entrepreneurship. She collaborates with NGOs, leverages her company's resources for broader educational access, and speaks at global forums about technology's role in education. Her career journey moved from survival success to fulfilment success on the Ladder of Growth.

Zoe: The Corporate Trailblazer

EARLY STAGE

- Zoe begins her career in finance at a multinational corporation. She's known for her analytical skills and innovative problem-solving approaches. Initially, Zoe focuses on excelling in her role, gaining certifications in financial analysis, and building a solid professional network.

MID STAGE

- Recognized for her expertise and leadership potential, Zoe is promoted to head the finance department. She faces the challenge of leading a team during an economic downturn. Zoe's growth involves developing soft skills, including emotional intelligence, crisis management, and team motivation. She participates in leadership development programmes and finds a mentor.

LATER STAGE

- After years of contributing to her company's success, Zoe is invited to join the board of directors. She also becomes an advocate for women in leadership. At this stage, Zoe focuses on governance, corporate strategy, and mentorship. She launches initiatives for women's leadership within her organization and serves on panels to share her insights on navigating corporate structures.

COMPARISON

- **Growth over time:** Both Maya and Zoe showcase significant personal and professional growth over time, adapting to new roles, challenges, and opportunities.
- **Adaptability and learning:** Their journeys highlight the importance of being adaptable, continuously learning, and expanding their skill sets to meet evolving career and personal goals.
- **Impact beyond personal success:** Both leaders eventually focus on making a broader impact—Maya through addressing educational disparities and Zoe by advocating for women in leadership.

These examples illustrate that growth is a dynamic and continuous process. Leaders can navigate their careers through various stages, facing challenges with resilience, and ultimately contributing to their fields and society in meaningful ways.

Let's consider another example of two corporate women leaders, Nina and Sarah, who have charted different paths in their growth journeys within the corporate world.

Nina: The Innovator in Tech

BACKGROUND

Nina began her career as a software engineer in a leading tech company. Her passion for technology and innovation quickly set her apart as a forward-thinking problem solver.

EARLY CAREER GROWTH

Nina focused on mastering technical skills and leading small project teams. She pursued certifications in emerging technologies and often led her team in adopting new tools and methodologies.

MID-CAREER TRANSITION

Recognizing the importance of understanding the business side of technology, Nina transitioned into a product management role. She leveraged her technical background to bridge the gap between the engineering teams and market needs, driving the development of successful products.

LEADERSHIP ROLE

Eventually, Nina became the CTO of a startup focused on artificial intelligence, where she led the company's product development and strategic direction. Her growth path was marked by a continuous pursuit of innovation and a commitment to translating technical capabilities into marketable solutions.

GROWTH PHILOSOPHY

Nina's growth journey emphasizes continuous learning, adaptability, and leveraging technical expertise to drive business innovation. She believes in staying at the forefront of technology trends and using that knowledge to create competitive advantages.

Sarah: The Corporate Strategist

BACKGROUND

Sarah started her career in finance, working as an analyst at a multinational corporation. Her analytical skills and strategic thinking quickly earned her recognition.

EARLY CAREER GROWTH

She pursued an MBA to deepen her understanding of business strategy and leadership. Post-MBA, Sarah took on roles that involved strategic planning and operations, helping her to understand the broader operational challenges that businesses face.

MID-CAREER SHIFT

Sarah transitioned into a role focused on corporate development, where she was responsible for identifying and executing acquisition opportunities. This role allowed her to shape the strategic direction of her company significantly.

LEADERSHIP ROLE

Sarah eventually became the CEO of a division within the corporation, where she implemented transformative strategies that drove growth and improved operational efficiency. Her leadership style is characterized by strategic foresight, decisive action, and a focus on long-term sustainability.

GROWTH PHILOSOPHY

Sarah's path highlights the importance of strategic thinking, financial acumen, and the ability to navigate complex corporate structures. She values the power of strategic planning and execution in achieving business objectives and driving corporate growth.

COMPARISON

While Nina's growth journey is defined by her technical expertise and innovation in the tech sector, Sarah's path demonstrates the impact of strategic leadership and financial acumen in a corporate setting. Both leaders showcase the diversity of growth paths in the corporate world, emphasizing different skill sets and philosophies towards achieving success.

These examples illustrate that there is no one-size-fits-all approach to leadership growth. Whether through innovation and technology, or strategic planning and execution, successful leaders can emerge from various backgrounds and experiences, each bringing their unique perspective and approach to driving business success.

SUMMARY

Success and Growth are interconnected yet intrinsically differ from each other.

SUCCESS	GROWTH
Outcome-oriented: Success is typically defined by the achievement of specific goals or objectives. For example, promotions, bonus rewards.	**Process-oriented:** Growth is about the journey and the process of improving or developing. It focuses on the progression over time. For example, learning a new skill.
External validation: Success often involves recognition or validation by others, such as awards, promotions, financial gains, or public acknowledgment.	**Internal and personal:** It involves personal development, learning, and self-improvement, acquiring new skills, expanding knowledge, and evolving attitudes and behaviours.
Variable and tangible: The definition of success can vary greatly from person to person. It is subjective and depends on individual values and goals. For example, buying a house, becoming a VP or CEO.	**Continuous and ongoing:** It's a continuous, lifelong process. It doesn't have a definitive endpoint; there's always room for further development.

Success Trap: This is a situation where people become overly focused on achieving traditional validation of success like titles, promotions, and rewards. Moving towards more personal measures makes growth more meaningful and fulfilling.

Momentum Map: Using your personal values and aspirations to create a growth map that works for you.

REFLECT: SELF-ASSESS: ACTION

Reflect what we just discussed in the chapter above and use the following four blockers to self-assess where you are on the growth journey and write out one action that you can take to invest in your growth.

Sustain	Shrink
What behaviours should you continue to practice? Positive behaviours that are working well for you. For example, utilizing internal programmes to upskill in your job.	What behaviours are not serving you well in networking? Habits that you want to see less of. For example, pursuing promotion as the only way to grow.
The behaviours I want to sustain are . . . _____ _____ _____ _____	The behaviours I want to shrink are . . . _____ _____ _____ _____

Discard	Amplify
What is not working well for you?	What behaviours that you currently demonstrate need to be practised more?
Getting rid of mindsets that aren't working for you at all.	Practices that you should do more of.
For example, looking at your career as a linear path.	For example, investing time in building skills and knowledge outside of work.
The behaviours I want to discard are . . .	The behaviours I want to amplify are . . .
_____	_____
_____	_____
_____	_____

Take Action

- What is your one practice that you will put into action to nurture your growth?

6

Nurturing Allyship

Looking back, I realize my initial struggles in the business head role stemmed from a limiting mindset about the 'requirements' of the job. As an R&D person, I believed that technical expertise and experience were the sole factors for advancement. The more you knew and the faster you made decisions, the more qualified you were to lead.

Carrying this mindset into the business role, I felt immense pressure to quickly learn about marketing, sales, and finance, areas I had limited experience in. This self-imposed pressure to become someone I wasn't led to significant stress and even impacted my health in those initial months.

Fortunately, I had a pivotal conversation with my mentor, my boss' boss. I shared with him my feelings of inadequacy and asked for his guidance.

His response was a revelation. 'Zinnia, if we needed someone solely for their expertise in marketing, sales, or finance, we wouldn't have chosen you. We saw your leadership potential and your ability to learn and grow beyond R&D. You don't need to be an expert in everything, just understand the business well enough to lead effectively. That's why you're here. Relax, be yourself, and leverage your existing strengths.'

Zinnia Rivera shared this story when she was telling us about a key ally during a challenging time in her career. Zinnia is a seasoned management consultant who is based in the Philippines. She leverages her business leadership experience to provide strategic guidance to her clients.

In all our chapters so far, you would have noticed that one of the key ingredients to a woman leader being successful is having allies. You would've also noted from the stories we've shared that the woman leaders made an effort to seek out and find their allies. Since our book is about taking charge of your career and doing what you can to grow it, our focus in this chapter is to help you (the woman leader) recognize and find the allies you need, both at the individual and organizational level.

We've also dedicated a small section to what organizations can do to support women thus becoming allies. We did this so that women can elevate the conversation within their organization and with key stakeholders to create change. We believe that both individuals and organizations play a role in creating the right ecosystem for allyship to thrive.

In the context of workplace dynamics, social movements, and efforts towards gender equality, the term 'allies' refers to individuals who support and advocate for a group even if they aren't members of that group, particularly when they hold a more privileged position in society or within organizational structures. They can come in the form of sponsors, mentors, coaches, or simply just colleagues.

Here, we are particularly interested in allies for women leaders in Asia. We think there are certain characteristics that make for a good ally. They are obviously supportive, but they also take the time to educate themselves about the issues, historical context, and systemic barriers. They hold themselves accountable for their actions and most importantly, they are agents of change.

Having both male and female allies is crucial for advancing gender equality and creating a more inclusive culture in the workplace. Each brings unique perspectives, experiences, and benefits to the table, addressing different facets of the challenges faced by women, especially in leadership roles.

Male Allies

You may have heard of the adage that behind every successful man is a woman. Yes, there is because she is taking care of his home, kids, and family. However, we found that there are also supportive men who are behind the successful women we interviewed, the male allies who empowered these women leaders to reach for the stars.

Allyship from men begins at home where women find that their fathers, brothers, and husbands provide unwavering support as advocates for women's education and career growth. Male allies can significantly impact the workplace too by contributing to its inclusive culture. Their actions impact broader societal norms because they actively support, advocate for, and work alongside women to foster equality and inclusivity.

In essence, male allies can significantly influence the trajectory of women's leadership and the creation of a more inclusive culture by leveraging their positions, challenging the status quo, and actively supporting the advancement of women. The collaboration between male allies and women leaders not only benefits women but also enriches organizations and societies by fostering diverse perspectives, innovation, and a more equitable distribution of power. This leads to creating a workplace where everyone, regardless of gender, has equal access to opportunities, support, and the chance to succeed.

Enlisting male allies

My professional journey has been deeply enriched by the guidance and support of remarkable mentors. Looking back, I recognize how many individuals played a crucial role in shaping my approach to leadership, decision-making, and action.

My early mentors at Unilever, primarily my bosses, provided invaluable foundational lessons. Maricelle Narciso, who later became the Philippines country manager for PepsiCo, instilled in me the importance of precision and humility, gently highlighting oversights, prompting me to learn from my mistakes with grace. Geocel Olanday pulled no punches as he pushed for delivery of targets. Angie de Villa Lacson, still an influence for Strategy, challenged my seemingly brilliant proposals with insightful questions, forcing me to refine my thinking.

The transition to C-level brought a new dimension to my leadership evolution. My CEO at Shangri-la Plaza, Victoria 'Viksi' Egan, who trusted me as COO, instilled the high standard of critical thinking required at the board level, as well as the responsibility for flawless execution through building a skilled team and delivering constructive criticism. The board of directors, especially Carlos 'Sonny' Dominguez, who later became the Philippines Secretary of Finance, honed my skill in managing dissent and herding sometimes disparate shareholder positions into alignment. Sonny took time for a one-on-one conversation on managing board dynamics on the day I was promoted to CEO, as Viksi moved to the UK to become Global CEO at Laura Ashley.

These early mentors provided a framework for critical thought and decisive action, laying the groundwork for my continued growth. My colleagues at Globe Telecom, especially as I led the company's push into the high-risk world of innovation investments via venture capital, became invaluable resources, bridging the spaces between my traditional industry roles, my startup experience, and the dynamic world of technology investing.

My current CEO, Ernest Cu, has been instrumental in broadening my leadership style. His directness, while challenging at times, sharpened in me the value of contrarian thought, conviction, and thorough preparation. Ernest is a great balance of corporate + investor + entrepreneur, and he taught me the critical importance of market-right timing, especially in the fast-paced environment of venture capital.

Throughout my journey, I've not only received valuable lessons but also fostered meaningful connections and lasting friendships. Staying in touch with early mentors like Maricelle, Angie, and Geocel, as well as more recent ones like Viksi and Sonny, allows me to keep benefitting from their wisdom, share new things I'm seeing, enjoy their company, and express my gratitude as I recount the lessons I've gleaned from their guidance.

The impact of these mentors extends far beyond my own success. I carry their teachings forward, sharing them with colleagues and emphasizing the importance of continuous learning and collaborative growth. My journey is a testament to the transformative power of mentorship, highlighting its ability to shape individuals and cultivate a culture of shared learning and success.

The narrative above is what Minette Navarrete, president at Kickstart Ventures Inc., Philippines, told us about the role that allies—male and female—played in her career. Minette is a seasoned leader who currently leads a team to invest globally, serves on the board of directors for a number of companies, and brings with her a very diverse range of experience spanning from online gaming to property management to the FMCG world.

↔

Finding male allies may not be easy, given the lack of awareness, societal stereotypes, and the narrative that makes men the enemy of women's progress. However, enlisting more male allies is a crucial step in fostering gender diversity and achieving equality in the workplace and beyond. You can tackle this pushback from men and find allyship from them in your workplace and personal life through these strategies:

Ask for support

- Articulate your needs by clearly explaining the specific help you require, whether it's mentorship, sponsorship, visibility opportunities, or simply a sounding board for ideas. Frame your request in terms of the overall goal or benefit for the project or company. This can help your ally understand the broader impact of supporting you.

Share experiences

- Openly share your experiences and the challenges you face as a woman in your field or workplace. Personal stories can be powerful in changing perspectives and fostering empathy amongst your allies.

Seek common ground

- Identify mutual goals and areas of interest that can serve as a foundation for collaboration. Demonstrating how gender diversity benefits everyone can motivate men to become allies.

Engage in discussions and initiatives

- If you are part of a network that focuses on women's growth, then invite men to participate in discussions and initiatives related to gender equality and diversity. Their active participation can invite them to actively contribute to actions that empower women leaders.

Acknowledge and reward allyship

- Recognize and appreciate the efforts of male allies. Public acknowledgment can encourage further allyship and motivate others to follow suit.

By employing these strategies, women can effectively engage men in the journey toward gender equality, leveraging their support to make significant strides in breaking down systemic barriers and fostering a culture of mutual respect and collaboration.

An article by Meg Warren titled 'Why women need male allies in the workplace—and why fighting everyday sexism enriches men too' highlights that allyship from men not only benefits women, but men too have a lot to gain.

> Men who were more likely to act as allies to women reported proportionately higher levels of personal growth and were more likely to say they acquired skills that made them better husbands, fathers, brothers and sons. This tendency suggests the possibility that being a male ally creates positive ripple effects that extend beyond the workplace.

A diverse allyship provides women with a more extensive network of support, mentorship, and resources. Female allies often offer guidance and support based on shared experiences, while male allies can open doors to different networks and opportunities, ensuring women have access to a broad spectrum of professional development resources.

The interaction between male and female allies fosters an environment of mutual growth and learning. It encourages individuals to challenge their assumptions, broaden their understanding of gender issues, and develop more empathetic and inclusive leadership skills. This type of learning benefits not just women but all members of the organization, as it promotes a more respectful and collaborative workplace culture. By leveraging the strengths, perspectives, and influence of both, organizations can accelerate progress towards a more equitable and supportive environment for everyone.

Female Allies

It's interesting to note that while we often hear about issues like the gender pay gap, funding disparities, and the 'boys club', I've observed a positive shift in recent years. Many successful women in leadership positions are actively creating space for other women at the table.

This support extends beyond just words. They offer guidance, make introductions, and champion other women's potential. It's inspiring to see this dedication to building bridges and fostering a more inclusive environment.

As a woman leader myself, I believe that giving back is essential. When we climb the ladder, it's crucial to reach down and help others rise alongside us. This collaborative approach is the key to bridging the gap and creating a truly equitable space for everyone.

These thoughts were shared by Anna Vanessa Haotanto, founder & CEO, Zora Health, who is an award-winning entrepreneur, investor, and thought leader in entrepreneurship, technology, and leadership in Singapore.

↔

Women championing each other at work is pivotal for fostering an inclusive, supportive, and empowering workplace environment. When women actively support one another, they contribute not only to individual success but also to the broader goal of achieving gender equality and creating a culture of collaboration and mutual respect.

You don't have to be a senior leader and you don't have to wait to become a C-suite to mentor other women leaders. As soon as you come into the workforce, you are a role model for hundreds of women who want to start working. As a woman leader, you have an important role to play. Here are a few ways you can ensure allyship:

Amplify Voices

- Actively amplify the voices of other women by endorsing their ideas in meetings and giving credit where it's due. If you notice a colleague being interrupted or overlooked, redirect the conversation back to her, make sure her ideas are heard. Share information about upcoming projects, roles, or meetings where a peer could contribute or shine.

Mentor and Sponsor

- Offer guidance, advice, and feedback to less experienced women in your organization. Sharing your own experiences and lessons learned can be incredibly valuable to someone navigating their career path. Actively advocate for other women's advancement and opportunities. Use your influence to ensure they're considered for promotions, challenging projects, and leadership roles.

Celebrate Achievements

- Publicly celebrate the achievements and milestones of women colleagues. Recognition can boost confidence and visibility, and it reinforces the value of contributions made by women in the workplace. We women are not great at promoting ourselves; it's easier when others do that for us, and we can do the same for others.

Create Support Networks

- Establish or participate in networks and groups for women within your organization. These can provide spaces for sharing experiences, advice, and support, as well as for fostering professional connections. Share resources, recommend courses, and support each other's growth initiatives. Create a safe space for open dialogue where women can openly discuss challenges and frustrations they're facing, and offer advice on how to overcome them. Sometimes the most comforting and encouraging thing is to know that others have faced similar challenges and have overcome them. Share your own stories of struggle and triumph.

Provide Constructive Feedback

- Women often receive less helpful feedback than men, and women may hesitate to give critical feedback to women for fear of eliciting an emotional response such as being defensive, taking the feedback personally, or being hurt. Offer honest, constructive feedback in a supportive manner. Feedback is essential for growth and development, and regular, constructive feedback can help women understand their strengths and areas for improvement.

Challenge Gender Biases and Inequalities

- Actively challenge and speak out against gender biases and inequalities when you see them. This includes addressing microaggressions, advocating for equitable policies, and supporting a culture that values diversity and inclusion.

Provide Support During Transitions

- Offer your support to women who are going through transitions, such as returning from maternity leave or changing roles. These can be particularly challenging, and having support can make a significant difference.

By championing each other in these ways, women leaders can create a ripple effect of empowerment and change within their workplaces. Such efforts contribute to breaking down barriers, lifting each other up, and paving the way for future generations of women leaders.

Successful women have the capacity to spread the success and elevate others. So, ask yourself the question: You have made it but how many women did you help? This is an important question because it's often remarked that women don't really support each other. We want to share some context to clarify where this assumption comes from.

Queen Bee Effect

The 'Queen Bee Effect' refers to a phenomenon where a woman in a position of authority in a male-dominated environment may distance herself from other women and may even be more critical or less supportive of them. This term originates from the behaviour of queen bees in a beehive, where there is typically only one dominant female that reigns over the others.

Authors of the book, *It's Not You It's the Workplace: Women's Conflict at Work and the Bias that Built It*, Andrea S. Kramer and Alton B. Harris say that during their research they didn't find any empirical evidence supporting the notion that women are more mean-spirited, antagonistic, or untrustworthy in dealing with other women than men are in dealing with other men.

Why Is This View So Prevalent?

Women leaders might sometimes feel pressured to adopt this stance due to the scarcity of leadership roles available to them, leading to a sense of competition rather than collaboration with other women. This is often a result of systemic issues within the organizational culture and the societal norms that put women in a position where they feel they must compete for limited opportunities.

In various Asian societies, there are deeply ingrained gender norms and expectations. Women are often socialized to be collaborative and nurturing, and when they ascend to leadership roles, they might encounter conflicting expectations. This dissonance between being soft spoken, consensus driven, and nurturing versus being a leader who leads from the front and is assertive can make women distance themselves from these feminine stereotypes.

Women, like men, can internalize societal biases about gender and they manifest in the way women show up in leadership roles. This could show up as adopting behaviours that align with traditional male leadership styles, or conversely, distancing themselves from other women who they perceive as embodying feminine stereotypes that are often undervalued in professional settings.

For some women, the Queen Bee Effect may be a defensive strategy. In environments where they have had to fight hard to establish their authority, they might perceive other women as threats, especially in settings where gender bias is prevalent. This behaviour may stem from a sense of needing to protect their hard-earned status.

The impact of the Queen Bee Effect is both on the women who exhibit this behaviour and on those around them.

Women who exhibit Queen Bee behaviours often find themselves isolated. This isolation can limit their ability to build supportive networks, which are crucial for long-term career success and personal growth. By distancing themselves from other women and possibly adopting more traditionally masculine behaviours, these leaders might inadvertently reinforce gender stereotypes and the notion that you have to behave like a man to succeed.

Engaging in such behaviours can lead to increased stress and internal conflict, especially if these actions are at odds with one's personal values or desired leadership style.

One of the crucial aspects of career advancement is mentorship, which may be lacking if senior women are not supportive of their junior counterparts. When women leaders do not support other women, it can contribute to the ongoing gender imbalance in leadership roles, particularly in sectors where women are already underrepresented. Lack of support from female leaders can contribute to a more competitive and less collaborative work environment, which can be demoralizing and hinder the professional growth of other women.

This phenomenon can be disheartening for aspiring female leaders, especially young women who may see fewer role models who are supportive of other women.

What Can You Do to Avoid Being the 'Queen Bee'?

The first step that one can take is to reflect on one's own behaviour and attitudes towards other women in the workplace. Recognizing any biases or competitive feelings is the first step towards change.

Establish and engage in mentorship programmes that connect women in leadership with female colleagues at various stages of their careers. Create or participate in networks and support groups for women within the organization. Recognizing and celebrating the achievements of female colleagues and creating opportunities for their growth and visibility can help mitigate competitive behaviours.

Work towards identifying and challenging organizational cultures and policies that may inadvertently promote competition or exclusion among women. Advocating for fair and transparent processes for promotion, recognition, and compensation can help create a more equitable environment.

Women in leadership positions can set a powerful example by actively supporting and advocating for other women. Demonstrating solidarity, empathy, and a commitment to gender equality can inspire others to do the same.

Now that we have addressed and talked about this phenomenon, we also want to acknowledge all the women who support and empower other women.

Women's Groups—Yay or Nay

Similar to the remark on women supporting women, we also want to address the role of women's groups and their effectiveness.

Despite similar goals of fostering connections, women's groups often face more criticism than men's networks ('boy's clubs'). Culture, history, and bias all influence how we view women's groups and men's networks. Women's groups are a response to exclusion, challenging the existing power structure. This can be seen as threatening by those who benefit from the status quo.

Since women's groups aim for equality, they are sometimes seen as divisive instead of necessary to overcome existing bias. In cultures with less emphasis on equality, women's groups may be met with resistance. Women's initiatives are often held to a higher standard than men's networks, facing more scrutiny and criticism. Stereotypes about women's groups can make them seem less effective or valuable than men's networks.

In an article in Forbes, 'Overcoming Challenges Together: The Benefits Of Women's Support Groups', Angela Chan highlights the importance of women's support groups. She says:

> Women's support groups offer a variety of benefits, including shared experiences, emotional support, practical advice, accountability, and a sense of community. It is essential to carefully evaluate the group's mission, values, leadership experience, member synergies, and the communities they serve.

As a woman leader, you play a pivotal role in changing perceptions about women-only groups, transforming them from being seen as exclusive or divisive to being recognized as empowering platforms that promote diversity, equity, and inclusion. You can publicly acknowledge and showcase the positive outcomes achieved by women who have benefited from participation in these groups. This demonstrates the tangible impact these groups can have on women's careers. Or you can demonstrate your personal commitment to these groups by actively participating in meetings, events, and mentorship programmes.

A few years back, I (Rajita) started my coach certification journey. The course wasn't just about the curriculum; it was about finding my tribe. Meeting these incredible women felt like coming home. We shared our challenges, celebrated victories, and confessed our fears in a space completely free of judgement. We championed each other every step of the way. Even today, our bond remains strong—a constant source of support and encouragement. This experience of true connection is exactly what women's groups offer. They're not just places to chat; they're vibrant communities where we uplift each other, forge paths forward together, and build a network that empowers each member to rise.

Women for women is a reminder that when we join hands, we're not just helping an individual, we're strengthening an entire community. Through every conversation, every shared struggle, and triumph, we're not only finding our allies but becoming them. In these spaces, we're all builders of bridges, making it a little easier for the next woman to cross over.

Organization as an Ally

There is no doubt that organizations play an outsized role in creating allyship for their women employees. Before we address what organizations can do, let's talk about the downsides of organizations not investing in women.

Women in Asian workplaces face numerous hurdles throughout their careers. Societal expectations prioritize family responsibilities, while male-dominated cultures and leadership structures create an invisible barrier for advancement. Limited access to professional networks and the pressure of a dual burden further hinder their progress. Cultural perceptions of leadership and re-evaluations of career goals mid-career can lead some women to step back or seek alternative paths, ultimately contributing to a lower number of women reaching senior leadership positions in Asia.

If organizations don't factor these in as they find ways to support women, and if they don't create the right environment, it is tough for women to strike the balance between their personal and professional lives. This leads to women leaders dropping out at various stages in their careers.

↔

Gigi Parco is a veteran leader who is now enjoying her stint as an on-call consultant. Gigi has had a long career leading organizations in the FMCG and logistics industries in the Philippines. She shares her story as an example of the many decisions she had to make to achieve balance throughout her career. These choices, guided by her personal values, have shaped her career path and continue to do so even in retirement.

Early in my career, I found myself pulled in two demanding directions: work and family. Becoming a new wife and mother a year after starting my first meaningful job was a whirlwind. The joy of my family was undeniable, but the pressure to succeed at work intensified.

Exhaustion became a constant companion. I felt guilty about spending too much time at the office and missing precious moments with my child. The guilt only worsened when my second child arrived, adding a demanding toddler to the mix.

At the time, remote work wasn't an option. The long hours and intense schedule of my trade marketing role, which I loved, were simply incompatible with my new reality. Faced with an impossible dilemma, I had a tough decision to make. I sat down with my husband, my biggest supporter, and we openly discussed solutions. We created a schedule to share childcare responsibilities, ensuring I got the sleep I desperately needed. We also explored the possibility of help from family or nannies, a common practice in Southeast Asia—where I lived.

However, the real turning point came when I approached my superiors. I explained my situation and requested a temporary position that would allow me to focus on my family without derailing my career. I emphasized my value to the organization and my desire for a long-term future there.

Unfortunately, the leaders weren't receptive to my request. The company culture at the time lacked understanding of the challenges faced by working mothers. This left me with a heartbreaking choice: my sanity and family, or my career aspirations.

I knew I had to prioritize my well-being. With a heavy heart, I tendered my resignation. It was a gamble, but I believed in my abilities and knew I could find a more supportive work environment.

A year later, my former company came knocking on my door. They acknowledged their mistake and offered me a promotion with some of the flexibility I craved. It was tempting, but I wasn't ready to compromise again. I politely declined but made my position clear. I wouldn't sacrifice my personal life for work but my dedication and work ethic remained strong.

This experience taught me the importance of setting boundaries. Finding a company culture that values both my professional and personal life became a core value in my career journey.

↔

It is helpful for organizations to understand why women are reluctant when it comes to reaching out to allies to ask for help, for access to opportunities for growth, or for exceptions and accommodations to balance their personal priorities with their work. Understanding these factors is crucial for organizations to address the underlying issues and foster an environment where women feel empowered to seek support.

The reluctance to reach out to their allies whether individual or organizational, for support in professional settings, especially in leadership roles, can be attributed to several interconnected factors. These factors stem from systemic issues, societal norms, and personal apprehensions, all of which influence the dynamics of seeking support. Let's look at some of the reasons why women may not seek allies at work.

Fear of Being Perceived as Weak or Incompetent

- In many Asian cultures, there's a strong emphasis on self-reliance and maintaining face, and asking for help or exceptions may be seen as a sign of weakness or incompetence. Many women worry that seeking help will be interpreted as a lack of capability or knowledge, undermining their competence and authority, especially in leadership positions. This concern is often amplified in male-dominated industries or roles where women feel they must prove themselves to be as much or more competent than their male counterparts.

- Seeking help may be perceived by some women as potentially reinforcing negative gender stereotypes, such as the idea that women are inherently less capable or more dependent than men. Women in leadership positions, in particular, might be cautious about anything that could be seen as undermining their authority and competence.
- Additionally, Imposter Syndrome or the persistent belief that one is not as competent as others perceive them to be, disproportionately affects women. This can lead to a fear that asking for help will expose them as a fraud or unworthy of their position, further discouraging them from seeking the support they need.

Fear of Burdening Others

- Many Asian cultures prioritize collectivism over individualism, where the needs and goals of the group are seen as more important than those of the individual. So, a woman leader may not voice her own needs as it comes in the way of the group's goals. The concern about being a burden to others can deter women from asking for help. They may worry about taking up colleagues' time or resources, especially in high-pressure environments where everyone is managing heavy workloads.
- Women might also hesitate to ask for help if they feel they cannot offer something in return, due to a sense of fairness or reciprocity. This is compounded in environments where competitive dynamics are encouraged over collaborative ones.

Lack of Accessible Role Models or Support Networks

- Women in leadership positions often find themselves in environments with few female role models or mentors. The absence of a supportive network or examples of other women openly seeking help can reinforce the idea that they should navigate challenges independently.
- Similarly, if male allyship is not visibly demonstrated or recognized within an organization, women may not be aware of which male colleagues are genuinely supportive and open to being approached for help. Without clear signals of allyship, it's challenging to know whom to trust and reach out to. Women may question whether their male colleagues will truly understand their perspectives or challenges, especially those related to gender.

Organizations can support women leaders by fostering inclusive cultures, facilitating access to networks and mentorship, and actively working to challenge and change traditional perceptions of leadership and gender roles. They can begin by taking basic steps like recognizing and celebrating the achievements of women at all levels of the organization or supporting the creation and activities of Employee Resource Groups (ERGs) specifically for women and their allies.

By creating an environment that supports the growth and advancement of women leaders, organizations can tap into a broader talent pool, and drive innovation and success in the competitive Asian markets.

When nurturing female talent in the organization, it is prudent that we understand the concept of equity versus that of equality. While often confused with each other, there is a stark difference between equity and equality. Equality offers the same resources to all, while equity recognizes different needs and tailors support to ensure everyone has an equal chance to succeed.

This distinction is vital for empowering women leaders, who may face unique challenges requiring specific resources to thrive. Organizations sometimes use the lens of equality when providing opportunity to all their employees. However, when it comes to providing the chance for women to thrive and grow in the organization, equity is the approach that's really required.

Here we list some actions that organizations can take to build an equitable infrastructure of allyship for women.

How Can Organizations Be Better Allies?

Invest in female talent

- Organizations today focus only on women with leadership potential. However, what they need to work on is to provide personalized development plans based on the bespoke needs of the women in the organization. This may include specialized training, rotational assignments across different functions, and challenging projects that stretch their capabilities and prepare them for growth in their careers.
- All women should have equal opportunities to lead projects that are critical to the organization's success. This visibility and exposure are essential for building their profiles and demonstrating their capabilities to senior leadership, thereby positioning them for advancement.

Ensure equitable compensation and benefits

- Conducting regular pay equity audits helps ensure that women are paid fairly relative to their male counterparts for similar roles and performance levels. Organizations should be transparent about how salaries are determined and make concerted efforts to address any identified pay disparities, demonstrating a commitment to equity.
- To support women in balancing professional and personal responsibilities, organizations should offer

flexible working arrangements, such as remote work, flexible hours, and part-time positions. Another factor is how organizations support the re-induction of women leaders post maternity-leave or any other long-term leave. Support for women who re-enter the workforce after a significant break is an often-ignored area for many companies.

Set and monitor diversity goals

- Setting clear, measurable goals for increasing the representation of women in leadership positions within the organization is crucial. Incorporating these goals into leaders' performance evaluations and linking them to incentives can drive accountability and progress towards achieving gender diversity in leadership.

- Organizations should regularly assess the effectiveness of their initiatives to support women leaders, seeking feedback from participants and reviewing diversity metrics. This ongoing evaluation enables organizations to identify areas for improvement and adapt their strategies to better meet the needs of women employees, ensuring that efforts to foster a pipeline of women leaders are effective and responsive to changing dynamics.

Implement leadership, mentorship, and sponsorship programmes

- Facilitating access to internal and external networking events, leadership forums, and professional development opportunities allows women to build valuable connections, learn from peers and industry leaders, and stay abreast of industry trends and best practices. These forums are crucial in helping find mentors and sponsors who can invest in their growth. Supporting continuous learning through educational sponsorships and access to training courses further enhances their skills and readiness for leadership roles.

- Mentorship and sponsorship are key to advancing women in their careers. Mentors provide guidance and advice, helping mentees navigate the workplace and develop professionally. Sponsors go a step further by actively advocating for their protégés' advancement and exposure. Both programmes should aim to match women with leaders who can help them grow, with an emphasis on training mentors and sponsors to address gender-specific challenges. We will deep dive into this later in the chapter.

Having shared all those strategies, we do recognize that supporting women leaders in Asia requires organizations to navigate a complex interplay of cultural, social, and economic factors. Here are some nuances that organizations need to be sensitized to:

Heterogeneity

- Asia is incredibly diverse, comprising various cultures, languages, and religions. Organizations should avoid a one-size-fits-all approach and instead tailor their support to the specific cultural context of each country and even within different regions of a country. For example, the legal frameworks governing gender equality and workplace discrimination vary widely across Asia. Organizations must navigate these differences to ensure they comply with local laws where they exist. That said, even if there are no formal laws or policies on gender equality in a county, it is imperative that organizations strive to maintain high standards for gender equality across all operations.

Cultural norms and expectations

- In many Asian cultures, business and professional advancement are heavily influenced by personal relationships and networks. Women may have fewer opportunities to enter these traditionally male-dominated networks.

Organizations can facilitate networking opportunities and mentorship programmes to help women build essential connections. Similarly, the social expectations from women when it comes to family responsibilities while similar across Asia, can be different in individual Asian countries. Therefore, having a deep understanding of local cultural nuances becomes important for organizations.

Varying levels of development

- Asia encompasses countries at vastly different stages of economic and social development. This diversity impacts educational opportunities, workforce participation rates for women, and the availability of support systems for women in leadership. Organizations should consider these factors when designing initiatives to support women leaders, meeting them where they are.

By being mindful of these nuances, organizations can more effectively support the development and advancement of women leaders in Asia. This requires a commitment to understanding the unique context of each country and region, as well as a dedication to creating inclusive, supportive environments that recognize and leverage the strengths of diverse working cultures.

Allyship in Action

We'd like to dig deeper into what we think are the two most powerful and easy to implement tools that organizations have at their disposal—mentorship and sponsorship. If used correctly, they play an important role in the advancement of women leaders.

In a *Harvard Business Review* article titled, 'A Lack of Sponsorship Is Keeping Women from Advancing into Leadership', the author, Herminia Ibarra, highlights the importance of having mentorship and sponsorship for women leaders. She goes on to say that, 'Having an executive-level sponsor can be make or break for a high-potential woman's career, particularly when it comes to getting important roles that are stepping-stones to the top.'

Even the stories from the women leaders we interviewed make the case stronger for organizations to invest in these low hanging opportunities.

Mentorship focuses on providing guidance, advice, and support. A mentor is someone who has walked the path before and can share insights and experiences to help a protégé or mentee navigate their own career journey.

For women leaders in Asia, mentorship can be particularly valuable in addressing unique cultural and societal challenges. Mentors can offer personal advice on overcoming gender biases, balancing professional and personal life, and developing leadership skills in environments that may traditionally favour male leaders. They can additionally bring in the cultural context that interplays with the workplace. Mentorship is often about personal and professional growth, focusing on the development of the individual.

↔

Ardelia Apti shared with us her story of how the mentorship programme that her organization put together really helped transform her career. Ardelia is part of the board of directors of Mapan, a company focusing on women empowerment and improving the lives of the lower-end segment through new income opportunities and financial access. She is based in Indonesia and is an experienced business leader in Indonesian tech companies/startups.

> Looking back, my time at a top management consulting firm was transformative, but it wasn't always easy. During my early days, my shyness and lack of confidence held me back, particularly when it came to communication. Even basic interactions felt like a daunting task.
>
> However, their unique culture ended up shaping me in a positive way. Their dedicated track for local university graduates wasn't about segregation; it was a path built with understanding. They recognized the specific needs of individuals like me, providing an environment where

we could adapt and adjust with extra support. This made me feel truly nurtured and welcomed.

Two key aspects of the company's approach significantly boosted my confidence and learning: their specialized training and genuine mentorship.

Firstly, the structured mentorship programme was unlike anything I'd experienced before. It wasn't just about attention or care, it was about meticulously understanding my strengths and weaknesses and then methodically building a path for improvement. This structured approach was invaluable.

Secondly, I learned the true meaning of mentorship here. My mentors weren't just project managers or development coaches; they genuinely cared about my professional growth. They invested time and effort in understanding me as a whole person, not just an employee. This focus on individual well-being and holistic development resonated deeply with me.

This experience heavily influenced my own leadership style and the values I hold dear in my company. We prioritize mentorship that views individuals as complete human beings, not just workers. It's not just about who can do what task well, but about building upon natural strengths and fostering a foundation of character and values. This approach encourages open communication, allowing people to acknowledge their limitations and celebrate their strengths.

Furthermore, I embrace the concept of 'strength-based learning'. It's not about excelling at everything, but about identifying and honing areas where you can truly shine. As a woman leader, this approach has been instrumental in building my own confidence. Mentoring others and witnessing their journeys has made me realize that self-compassion is essential for both personal and professional growth.

Ultimately, my experience at this top management consulting firm taught me the importance of tailored support, genuine mentorship, and a holistic approach to development. These principles are core values I strive to embody as a leader and instil within my own company.

↔

Sponsorship on the other hand, is more about advocacy and opening doors. Sponsors are typically people in positions of power who use their influence to actively advocate for an individual's career advancement. They might recommend their protégé for opportunities, introduce them to key networks, and endorse their skills and capabilities to others. For women in Asia, where leadership roles may not be as readily accessible due to gender stereotypes or hierarchical corporate cultures, having a sponsor can be a game-changer. Sponsors not only believe in the potential of the individual but also take active steps to ensure their talents are recognized and rewarded at the decision-making table.

↔

Dr Vinika Rao started her career with a multinational bank in India, and is currently the executive director of INSEAD Africa Initiative and Hoffmann Institute for Business & Society, Asia, and an adjunct professor at INSEAD and SMU. She also sits on several boards and advisory boards and advises international organizations on DEI and ESG. Her research interests include gender diversity in corporate leadership, male allyship, millennials and multigenerational influences in the workplace, and emerging market strategies. Dr Rao shared with us excerpts of her research on sponsorship and how it shaped her career too.

> While mentorship is undoubtedly important, and I'm fortunate to have had and continue to have amazing mentors, I believe sponsorship takes things a crucial step further. Mentorship offers guidance and support, but sponsorship adds an element of advocacy and active promotion.

Many women are already highly qualified and capable; they're not aiming for something beyond their reach. What they often need is that 'extra push', that recognition of their potential, that can be less frequent for women due to systemic biases.

Women's networks are a great platform for connection and sharing, but true progress lies in engaging men as active allies within these networks. By listening to the concerns and talents highlighted in these meetings, men can take concrete actions. This could involve making introductions for suitable candidates for open positions, recommending relevant development opportunities (like courses or experiences) to fill identified gaps in profiles, and actively advocating for women within their networks.

This active intervention goes beyond simply saying, 'This opportunity might be good for you.' It's about providing tangible support, guidance, and opportunities. While mentorship plays a valuable role, sponsorship involves going the extra mile to level the playing field.

Furthermore, I firmly believe that sponsorship efforts need to be measurable. Just like 'what gets measured gets done' applies to businesses, setting clear Key Performance Indicators (KPIs) for sponsorship programmes holds leaders accountable for achieving gender balance, racial balance, or overcoming any existing imbalances within their organizations.

Ultimately, research consistently shows that leaders play a critical role in fostering a truly inclusive environment. This involves more than just policies and procedures; it requires leaders who demonstrate genuine commitment, openly acknowledge and address their own biases, display humility, and embrace collaboration. These qualities are essential for fostering effective sponsorship and creating a truly inclusive workplace for everyone.

↔

To summarize, mentorship helps in building the capabilities and resilience needed for leadership, while sponsorship ensures those qualities are seen and valued by others, opening doors to advancement and leadership opportunities. The main difference lies in their approach and impact—mentorship is about advising and supporting, whereas sponsorship is about advocating and facilitating opportunities.

Both are essential for overcoming the glass ceiling effect and ensuring women leaders in Asia can navigate their paths to success with confidence.

What Can You Do to Nurture Allies?

Gaining allyship, particularly for women in leadership roles, involves cultivating a supportive network that includes both men and women. This approach is not about rewriting the rules as much as it is about enhancing strategies to build meaningful, supportive relationships that foster mutual growth and understanding.

↔

Uma Thana Balasingam—the founder & CEO of the Lean In Network, Singapore, and ELEVATE—shared her approach to finding allies.

> Mentorship is a powerful tool for growth, and having a diverse board of mentors can be incredibly valuable. This isn't just about formal relationships with labelled titles; it can be a casual conversation with your CFO offering financial advice—a subject-matter mentor in action.
>
> I've embraced ten different types of mentors, including those younger and older than me, subject matter experts, and even health mentors. But if you're just starting out, here's a simple approach to finding your first mentor:

Identify your needs

- Start by pinpointing your current challenge. Forget the five-year plan; focus on the immediate hurdle. For example, if you want to boost your visibility, find individuals you admire who excel in that area.

Make the connection

- Don't just ask someone to be your mentor, especially if you don't know them. Instead, reach out and express your admiration. Briefly mention their work you found particularly impressive (one sentence is enough!) and then ask for a short meeting to discuss how you can improve your visibility.

Remember, humans help humans

- Don't underestimate the power of human connection. We all enjoy helping others, and reaching out demonstrates initiative and respect.

Following up is key

- After the meeting, send a thank-you note and mention any additional questions you may have. This keeps the conversation going and demonstrates your genuine interest.

Nurture the relationship

- This thirty-minute meeting can evolve into a long-term mentorship if nurtured. As new questions arise, reach out again and suggest another brief chat.

Her words of wisdom really are the essence of what women can do to find the allies they need to grow in their career.

↔

While organizational support is important, relying solely on it can be limiting. Broadening your network beyond your immediate organization to include industry groups, professional associations, and informal networks can offer diverse perspectives, opportunities, and support systems. This external network can be particularly valuable during transitions or when seeking unbiased advice.

This shift from passive to active engagement in one's career and leadership journey encourages women to take control of their growth, visibility, and networks, foster an environment where they can thrive as leaders, and build a supportive community around themselves. Adopt these strategies to navigate the challenges of leadership with confidence and resilience, paving the way for a more inclusive and empowering future.

We also wanted to outline how, when you work on elements from each of the 'rules', you can build the allyship you seek.

SUMMARY

Confidence

- **Embrace authenticity:** Be true to your values, beliefs, and leadership style. Authenticity resonates with people and naturally attracts allies who appreciate and support your genuine self.
- **Communicate assertively:** Clear, confident communication about your goals, needs, and expectations can help others understand how they can support you.

Visibility

- **Share your achievements:** Don't shy away from showcasing your successes and contributions. Visibility is crucial for building your personal brand and attracting allies who recognize your value and are willing to support you.
- **Engage in cross-functional projects:** Increase your visibility across different parts of the organization or community by participating in or leading projects that require cross-functional collaboration.

Networking

- **Build strategic relationships:** Actively seek connections with individuals who share your professional interests or support your growth. This includes reaching out to both men and women who can offer different perspectives and support.
- **Offer support:** Allyship is a two-way street. Be willing to support others in their goals and challenges. This builds trust and reciprocity, encouraging others to support you in return.

Balance

- **Foster inclusive environments:** Advocate for and contribute to environments that value diversity and inclusion. Encourage open discussions about gender equity and support policies that benefit everyone, not just women.
- **Practice empathy:** Understand the challenges and perspectives of others. Empathy can bridge gaps between different experiences and backgrounds, fostering a sense of mutual support and understanding.

Success

- **Mentorship and sponsorship:** Seek mentors and sponsors and be willing to mentor others. These relationships can provide guidance, open doors to new opportunities, and strengthen your network of allies.
- **Encourage continuous learning:** Promote a culture of learning and development that benefits all team members. Encourage both men and women to pursue growth opportunities, demonstrating your commitment to collective success.

We want to close this chapter with another powerful story that one of our women leaders, Geeta Singh, shared about how having the right allies at crucial junctures of their career helped them grow.

↔

Geeta is a seasoned HR leader with over twenty-five years of experience across Tech, Consulting, Telecom, and Financial Services. She is currently based in Singapore, and has worked in both regional (Asia Pacific, Europe, Middle East, and Africa) and global leadership roles.

One impactful example is my former boss. There was a leadership role in Singapore that opened up about ten years ago. While I was interested in career growth, I was hesitant to move out of India, where I had my family. Previously, I had declined relocation offers to the US for the same reason.

My boss recognized my potential and gently nudged me to consider the Singapore opportunity. She emphasized that applying wouldn't be a commitment in itself, and encouraged me to keep an open mind and explore the possibilities. This freed me from pressure and allowed me to approach the interview process comfortably.

I got the role and decided to take it. However, I expressed my desire to return to India after a period of building the team there. My boss was receptive and committed to working out a plan for my transition back if I decided to come back.

The two years turned out to become ten-plus years, and that single decision changed the course of my career and its growth.

This experience highlighted to me the importance of allies who see your potential and encourage you to explore opportunities, even if they require stepping outside your comfort zone.

Another aspect of having allies, I realized, is in building a network of strong relationships within your organization. In a global company like Google, progress often relies on relationships, not just individual work. This is where network allies come in. These aren't necessarily people you work with directly, but colleagues you've built trust with over time. They respect your judgement, value your contributions, and may even be peers. I've been fortunate to have peers who shared a sense of mutual respect and collaboration. We prioritized the organization's best interests over individual gain, allowing us to work together effectively.

When building allies, while it's tempting to connect with influential individuals, it's crucial to maintain alignment with your own values.

Finally, allies can also be project-specific. In an organization like Google, decisions often require consensus, and these allies can help move things forward by leveraging their position within the organization.

By recognizing different types of allies and fostering these relationships, I've been able to navigate challenges, explore opportunities, and ultimately achieve success in my career.

REFLECT: SELF-ASSESS: ACTION

Reflect what we just discussed in the chapter above and use the following four blockers to **self-assess** where you are on the growth journey and write out one **action** that you can take to nurture allyship.

Sustain	Shrink
What behaviours should you continue to practice? Positive behaviours that are working well for you. For example, being upfront about the kind of support you're looking for.	What behaviours are not serving you well? Habits that you want to see less of. For example, thinking that you may be burdening someone when you ask for help.
The behaviours I want to sustain are . . . _____ _____ _____ _____	The behaviours I want to shrink are . . . _____ _____ _____ _____

Discard	Amplify
What is not working well for you? Getting rid of mindsets that aren't working for you at all. For example, competing with women instead of collaborating.	What behaviours that you currently demonstrate need to be practised more? Practices that you should do more of. For example, raising your hand up to be an ally.
The behaviours I want to discard are . . .	The behaviours I want to amplify are . . .
_____ _____ _____ _____	_____ _____ _____ _____

Take Action

- What is your one practice that you will put into action to nurture allyship?

Conclusion

Own It!

Wrapping up *ReWrite the Rules* has been quite the journey. We've dived into the lives and lessons of some incredible Asian women leaders, hoping to pass on their stories and insights to you—our next wave of trailblazers.

This book is special because of the heartfelt conversations we had with these women about their hurdles and challenges and how they overcame them despite all odds. It is a culmination of all the stories we heard from hundreds of women across all countries in Asia, and while you may not see all of them in the book, we know that this book wouldn't have been possible without the generosity of wisdom of all the women we spoke to.

From the start, we wanted this book to feel like a chat with mentors or other kindred spirits who have traversed the same journey our readers are on—from tackling self-doubt to stepping into the limelight to forging connections and finding that elusive balance.

Using the immeasurable power of stories, we've shared their experiences, challenges, and wisdom in the form of our key pillars.

- **Confidence:** Tackle that inner voice of doubt. Remember, confidence is like a muscle—the more you use it, the stronger it gets.
- **Visibility:** Shine a light on yourself and make yourself seen. Step out and own your space.
- **Networking:** Spend time building real, meaningful relationships and connections that can lift you up.
- **Balance:** Learn how to manage your energy to be the best version of yourself in everything you do.
- **Success:** Invest time in learning and evolving as you climb the ladder of growth.

When we started writing this book, we had no idea what impact it would have on us as authors. However, we began noticing a shift in how we were conversing and in our daily interactions at work. We knew that if we didn't walk our talk, we weren't being authentic.

Perhaps naively, we hadn't always been conscious of how our gender identity might shape our experiences. Writing this book helped us reflect more on the concept of gender and its impact. We began to acknowledge and value the lived experiences of other women regardless of whether or not it was something we had experienced ourselves.

As women who are from Asia ourselves, we see this book as a reminder of the Asian cultural fabric and its impact on the workplace. We wrote the book because there are steps each woman leader in Asia, with tools of reflection, assessment, and commitment, can take to succeed despite those barriers. She can write the rules that work for her rather than follow the traditional rules written by someone else. This book acknowledges that we're all on different paths and in different stages of our careers and lives and allows you to follow what resonates for you.

We also recognized that the onus cannot be on women alone and it takes an entire ecosystem to change and align to support women's growth, and this book is our small part in the much bigger movement towards achieving gender equality and creating equitable organizations.

As we were writing the book, we were heartened to see that Harvard economist Claudia Goldin was awarded the 2023 Nobel Prize in Economics for her work examining the gender pay gap. Amongst other reasons, her research shows that women are paid less than men on average despite having higher education levels and that most of the gap appears after childbirth. The recognition of her work made us doubly sure that we were on the right track with our mission to provide the support women need to succeed at work.

Through *ReWrite the Rules* we've embarked on a shared journey, but the conversation doesn't end here. It's merely the beginning of countless more dialogues, actions, and transformations. Let's keep the exchange going, keep questioning, and, of course, keep rewriting the rules.

If there are stories that you want to share with us, drop us a note at write@letsrtr.com.

Our rally cry for all the women out there is to rewrite your rules, take charge of your careers, and **own it!**

Notes to My Younger Self

On our podcast, *ReWrite The Rules*, we asked our guests what advice they would give their younger selves. Their answers were powerful, and as we listened, a fascinating pattern emerged. Their wisdom naturally aligned with our five key pillars: confidence, visibility, networking, balance, and success.

Get ready to be inspired by their words . . .

'Looking back, I realize I could have been much kinder to myself. When I was younger, there was this constant pressure to do more, to achieve more. It felt like there were endless expectations, and I often felt like I could have done better.'

'I've come to realize the importance of slowing down, both in life and in my career. Pushing too hard can make you miss the beauty of the journey. When faced with a challenge, the natural instinct is to accelerate and escape. Taking a step back, reflecting, and then moving forward strategically is a much wiser approach.'

'Learn to truly embrace yourself. It's about pushing boundaries, understanding your strengths, and leveraging them fully. Don't get caught up trying to follow someone else's path—this is your life, and you get to define it on your own terms. No one else gets to dictate your journey.'

'Beyond technical skills, teamwork is essential. Success is rarely achieved alone. Being a team player not only enhances your abilities but also fosters empathy for your colleagues and stakeholders.'

'That's why I tell young people not to chase passion blindly. Find something you're good at and bring passion to that. Passion isn't just about loving something; it's about applying an energetic and positive attitude to whatever you do.'

'When you start a new job at any company, it's crucial to identify what unique value you can offer. Every organization has different needs and opportunities. Your goal is to find a niche that both addresses those needs and aligns with your skills.'

'Don't be afraid to reinvent yourself. This keeps things exciting and prevents stagnation, which makes me genuinely happy to get up and go to work every day.'

'Speak up! Communicate openly about finances with your partner. It's a team effort and sharing the responsibility can create a more secure and stable foundation for your family.'

'Looking back, I'd tell my younger self to be patient. I used to be incredibly impatient with myself, wanting quick results. But many things take time. Learn to be patient and surround yourself with good people who will support and lift you up.'

'One piece of advice I've learned the hard way is, "never complain, never explain." It sounds harsh, but for me, it means focusing on self-improvement rather than dwelling on negativity. As a leader, you can't please everyone, and there will always be critics.'

'Looking back on starting my own business, one thing I really wish I'd done differently is having active co-founders. It was simply overwhelming. This experience taught me the crucial importance of having a support system, a "tribe" you can rely on. Founding a business can be romanticized, but it shouldn't come at the expense of your well-being.'

'Don't be afraid to stand out! Often, we feel pressure to conform in order to be included. But that's not true inclusion. Inclusion means being valued for who you are and what you bring to the table, even if your perspective is different.'

'Be confident in yourself and your ideas. Speak up! Having a unique point of view is valuable, and staying silent weakens your voice.'

'Looking back, I'd tell my younger self to embrace fun and exploration. Don't be afraid to fail—sometimes it's the best teacher. And most importantly, be courageous! Take on challenges, volunteer for new projects, and push your boundaries. Don't shy away from opportunities to contribute and make a difference.'

'Embrace boldness in leadership. It may not come naturally at first, but it's a valuable trait. Bold leadership doesn't mean sacrificing empathy or compassion. It's about finding the balance between decisiveness and compassion.'

'Be kind to yourself. It's okay not to be perfect. You don't have to constantly prove yourself to others. Prove yourself to your yesterday's self—strive to be a little better each day.'

'Don't be afraid to rest when you're tired. I wish I had done that more. Forgive yourself for mistakes, even those made out of ignorance. Seeking help isn't a sign of weakness; it's a sign of strength.'

'Back then, I felt like asking for help might make me seem weak or dependent. Now, I see it differently. Asking for help can save you time, prevent mistakes, and ultimately make you stronger.'

'Don't over plan or be a perfectionist. Life rarely unfolds exactly as planned.'

'Early in my career, I was afraid to ask for help, and that led me to leave organizations where I could have thrived. Don't make the same mistake! Embrace collaboration and seek out guidance when needed.'

'Have patience. Our digital world often breeds an expectation of instant results. But real-world problems often take time to solve. Believe in yourselves! Don't be afraid of calculated risks. You don't need 100 per cent confidence to go for a job or pursue an opportunity.'

'Hang in there! I've been there myself, feeling like I just couldn't do it anymore. Challenges at work, no matter how tough, are temporary. The key is to stay engaged and avoid feeling overwhelmed.'

'My most important advice? Don't get overwhelmed. Take a deep breath, break down large tasks into smaller chunks, and focus on progress, not perfection. Remember, this is just a phase, not your entire life.'

'Ask more questions. Don't rush for answers. As a younger person, I often felt pressure to have all the solutions. But sometimes, the most valuable thing you can do is ask thoughtful questions and sit with the uncertainty a little longer.'

'The answers often come unexpectedly. Don't force solutions. Take a walk, cook a meal. Sometimes the answer pops into your head while doing something mundane. The key is to be deliberate in your learning and committed to growth. Trust that the answer will come eventually.'

'Be prepared for scepticism, even from loved ones. If you've planned carefully, made intentional decisions, and taken accountability, then their doubts shouldn't deter you. It won't be perfect, but nothing ever is.'

'Ask for help! For most of my twenties and thirties, I mistakenly thought I needed to do everything alone. What I wish I knew then is this: people who want the best for you will be happy to help. My fear of seeming incompetent held me back.'

'Start building your network early. It may not come naturally to introverts, but visibility is key to career advancement. Plant the seeds early on, even if it's just making a small effort to connect with colleagues. Remember, people who want the best for you will be happy to help.'

'Embrace continuous learning. Don't become stagnant in your career. Always seek opportunities to develop new skills and knowledge, regardless of your seniority.'

'Cultivate your personal brand. We all have a unique value proposition—what makes you stand out? It's not just about technical skills; it's about your reputation, image, and how others perceive you.'

'I'd tell my younger self to take it easier. Don't sacrifice your well-being by neglecting sleep or meals. From the beginning, focus on creating a healthy balance— physically, mentally, spiritually, and emotionally. This will help you avoid burnout.'

'Looking back, the biggest advice I'd give my younger self is to be kinder. I used to be incredibly critical of myself, always striving to be the best. While I'm happy with my achievements, the journey could have been smoother with more self-acceptance.'

Inspired by these snippets? Scan the QR code to listen to the complete interviews and gain a wealth of actionable advice.

Acknowledgements

To my son Samar and daughter Nandini, thank you for your bright spirit and infectious optimism that constantly reminds me to lead by example.

I want to thank my husband, Gagan, who has been my greatest ally throughout my journey. Your unwavering support and belief in my vision has been the bedrock of my strength and perseverance.

—Ritu G. Mehrish

I am here because of the rock-solid support of so many incredible people in my life. A special shout out to my male allies—Air Commodore R. Raghuram, thank you for your invaluable mentorship during a critical career decision. Dr N.S. Prasant, your constant encouragement fuelled my confidence throughout my journey. Dr Uday Saxena, Dr Tarun Saxena, Mohammed Qader, Dilip Kumar, and BB Saxena, your belief in me, especially during life's challenges, has been instrumental in shaping who I am today. Also, Sanjay Saxena and Prakash Singh Bisht for infusing music and yoga into my life—they continue to enrich my life's journey.

You are all true leaders, and I am incredibly grateful for your enduring support.

—Rajita Saxena

To our collaborators & partners

Nora Nazerene Abu Bakar and the incredible team at Penguin Random House SEA: your collaborative spirit and expert guidance were instrumental in elevating this manuscript. Your expert guidance challenged us to refine our thoughts and express our vision with even greater clarity. Thank you for believing in this book and working side-by-side to share it with the world.

Aayushi Deshpande, your artistic talent transformed the book with captivating visuals. Beyond that, your early read of the draft and thoughtful suggestions were instrumental in making this book the best it can be. We are incredibly grateful for your creative partnership and support.

Ocean Reeve (Ocean Reeve Publishing), our deepest gratitude for being a wise advisor during the book's conception phase. Your early guidance helped us solidify the core ideas that would become the foundation of this work.

Danielle Goodman (The GoodGood Editing), your intervention was a turning point. Your thought-provoking questions and insightful advice were instrumental in bringing our vision to life.

The team at Crazytok Media—Amit Ray, Debangshu Paul, Shubhojit Ghosh, Tiasha Chatterjee, Athirupa Manichandar, and Ayu Latifah—deserves special recognition for their contribution. You helped us create an engaging podcast series and insightful newsletters to amplify the message of *ReWrite The Rules* and reach a wider audience.

Andy Greenway, Gerard Lim, Shen Au, and Abigail Low at Rumble for crafting the powerful branding for *ReWrite The Rules*. Your creative vision perfectly captured the essence of our book, and we are thrilled to share it with the world.

To the women who are rewriting the rules

This book would not have been possible without the generosity of the women leaders who not only gave us their time but also shared their stories with complete honesty and vulnerability.

It's been our honour and privilege to amplify your voices and share your wisdom with the world.

Ami Moris Dato, Anna Vanessa Haotanto, Aarti Dabas, Ardelia Apti, Arpita Pal Agrawal, Deepthi Bopaiah, Dr. Vinika Rao, Fanny Huang, Geeta Singh, Gigi Parco, Gloria Ngooi, Lay Peng Ong, Meera Vasudevan, Minette Navarrete, Nawan Poovarawan, Nicole Tan, Nora Nazerene Abu Bakar, Patricia Lin Feria, Pei Len Cho, Pratima Amonkar, Prof. Sun Sun Lim, Rachanee Chanawatr, Rejina Rahim, Sasibai Kimis, Uma Thana Balasingam, Zalina Jamaluddin, and Zinnia Rivera.

To the incredible women across Asia

Your voices, from surveys, brief conversations, and even casual chats, have been an invaluable part of this journey. We're deeply grateful for your contributions. Your insights and life experiences helped shape this book in profound ways.

Abigail Low	Jintao Guo	Pratima Bellave Ganesh
Aditi Das Patnaik	JK Lakshmi	Priyanka Vyas Agarwal
AiChen Wang	Joanne Chng	Qurrota A'Yunina
Aishwarya Pradeep	Jolene Hui Lin Koh	Rachel Foster
Ramappa	Joyce Yee	Rashi Srivastava
Akanksha Saxena	Julia Chua	Rashmi Parvathy
Alka Kaul	Kali Priya	Ratha Letchimanan
Amelia Kyle	Kanika Bansal	Reetika Ghai
Ammie Currie	Kavita Ganesh	Rekha Chigurupati
Amrita Khadilkar	Kavitha Elizabeth	Rekha Karthikeyan
Angie Paku	Metla	Resmito Rinie
Anita Yang	Kavitha Panasa	Richa Dua
Anju Patwardhan	Keerthi Vobhilineni	Rohini Rao
Anna Joke Breimer	Kim Dung Bui	Roszalena Mohammed
Bharti	Kristeen Henderson	Mashrudin
Anu Gupta	Laila Jailaty	Sabrina Xu
Anuradha Rao	Latha Gopalakrishnan	Saman Kazmi
Anusooya Devi	Lauren Marie Lee	Santosh Dobhal
Archana Sali	Lesley Powell	Sarah Najdek
Arpana Sali	Lien Tam Nguyen	Sarah Philippart
Ashna Kedia	Lien Vu	Saumya Mittal
Audrey Hong Kei Teoh	Liliana Mata	Sharon Sontillano
Avni Martin	Lisa Chua	Sheela Vatsala

Ayesha Thakkar
Bao Doris Qihui
Brigette Cias
Celine Nguyun
Chaithra Somashekar
Challika
Pothisarattana
Christina Wong
Christy Kim Velez
Deepika Sridhar
Diana Diana
Dipti Rao Dhar
Domini Genene Tamayo
Donna Smart
Donna Wilson
Dr Sushmita Sharma
Dr. Shashikala Singh
Elain Chee Vi Ling
Elaine Hollmann-
Haren
Elena Chan
Elfani Sari
Erica Cruz
Fareeha Khaleel
Fei Chen
Fiza Malhotra
Flora Young
Freeda Fernandes
Grace Leonor
Hecelyn Morente
Helena Rose Day
Ilze Nel
Ines Choi
Irma Lestari Silaban
Jacqui Reed
Jamuna Varghese
Jasmin Cruz
Jennifer Yu
Jingjin Liu

Lisa Kusuma
Liza Joseph
Lopamudra Ray
Madhu Saxena
Marrisa Bautista
Mayumi Marumo
Megha Golechha
Meghana Rajeshwar
Meghna Saxena
Melisha Ann See
Miah Shelford
Michelle Poh
Mizue Nakajima
Navreet Kaur
Nayana Cariappa
Nazratul Annis
Nidhi Gupta
Nikitha Fernandes
Nina Chandiramani
Saxena
Nupur Saxena
Kulshrestha
Olivia Ludlow
Pallavi Chanda
Saxena
Parul Garg
Pattama Sirichampa
Pavya Kavukalai
Payal Pisal
Peenaz Choksi
Pei chen Shieh
Piyanan Jaranupap
Pooja Dayal
Pooja M Chhangani
Pooja Sinha
Pramila Naniwadekar
Preeti Tiwari
Preeti Tyagi

Shen Au
Shenglan Cao
Shibani Sen
Shruti Kamath
Simone Tan
Sindhu Varghese
Sin Niew Loh
Siriwan Maneeratanaporn
Skylar Chou
Sneha Srinivasan
Sonali Kumar
Songyi Song
Sudarshana Bharadwaj
Sudha Mehta
Sudheshna Gupta
Sukanya Ghosh
Susan Leong
Tamara Ho
Tanvi Sharma
Thanattha Sirisaratanon
Thipapan Ployhin
Tifa Chueh
Tomoko Sakata
Tripa Basavaraj
Urvashi Bajpai
Urvi Jain
Varsha Singh
Veda Srinivasan
Vinita Khatter
Visha Chauhan
Vita Megawati
Xing Hui Oh
Xuqian Zhang
Yizhao Zhang
Zaidah Ibrahim
Zhaoru Zheng

Finally, we want to acknowledge multiple male allies who have played significant roles in our respective careers and lives, and those who boldly shared their inputs as we were writing the book.

References

6 ways that women can champion each other at work – Lean in. (n.d.). Lean In. https://leanin.org/tips/workplace-ally

Abdou, A. (2021, August 6). *The 2 types of confidence, according to science (and how to harness them).* LADDERS. https://www.theladders.com/career-advice/the-2-types-of-confidence-according-to-science-and-how-to-harness-them

Achor, S. (2019, November 22). *Do women's networking events move the needle on equality?* Harvard Business Review. https://hbr.org/2018/02/do-womens-networking-events-move-the-needle-on-equality

Aitsi-Selmi, A. (2020). *The success trap: Why Good People Stay in Jobs They Don't Like and How to Break Free.* Kogan Page Publishers.

Arscott, C. H. (2023, July 27). *A better approach to networking.* Harvard Business Review. https://hbr.org/2022/11/a-better-approach-to-networking

Arussy, L. (2015, June 1). *How to avoid falling into the "Success trap": Remember Circuit City? Pan Am? Borders Books? Blockbuster? There is a big difference between success and sustainable success.* Inc. https://www.inc.com/lior-arussy/success-may-be-your-biggest-obstacle-to-future-success.html

Castrillon, C. (2019, March 10). *Why women need to network differently than men to get ahead.* Forbes. https://www.forbes.com/sites/carolinecastrillon/2019/03/10/

why-women-need-to-network-differently-than-men-to-get-ahead/

Chin, S., Krivkovich, A., & Nadeau, M. (2018, September 6). *Closing the gap: Leadership perspectives on promoting women in financial services.* McKinsey & Company. https://www.mckinsey.com/industries/financial-services/our-insights/closing-the-gap-leadership-perspectives-on-promoting-women-in-financial-services

Coleman, J. (2022, January 11). *Finding Success Starts with Finding Your Purpose.* Harvard Business Review. https://hbr.org/2022/01/finding-success-starts-with-finding-your-purpose

Elsesser, K. (2020, August 31), Queen bees still exist, but it's not the women we need to fix. *Forbes.* https://www.forbes.com/sites/kimelsesser/2020/08/31/queen-bees-still-exist-but-its-not-the-women-we-need-to-fix/

Field, E., Krivkovich, A., Kügele, S., Robinson, N., & Yee, L. (2023). Women in the Workplace 2023. *McKinsey & Company.* https://www.mckinsey.com/featured-insights/diversity-and-inclusion/women-in-the-workplace

Stobierski, T. (2019, December 4). *How Leaders develop and use their network | HBS Online.* Business Insights Blog. https://online.hbs.edu/blog/post/importance-of-networking-in-leadership

Klinghoffer, D. (2023, February 6). *Hybrid Tanked Work-Life Balance. Here's how Microsoft is trying to fix it.* Harvard Business Review. https://hbr.org/2021/12/hybrid-tanked-work-life-balance-heres-how-microsoft-is-trying-to-fix-it

Lupu, I. & Ruiz-Castro, M. (2021, January 29). *Work-Life balance is a cycle, not an achievement.* Harvard Business Review. https://hbr.org/2021/01/work-life-balance-is-a-cycle-not-an-achievement

Networking doesn't have to be a drag. (2020, April 10). Harvard Business Review. https://hbr.org/podcast/2019/10/networking-doesnt-have-to-be-a-drag

Parmelee, M. (2023, June 16). *Empowering women at work.* Deloitte Insights. https://www2.deloitte.com/us/en/insights/topics/talent/work-life-balance-for-women.html

Paulise, L. (2023, August 3). 75% of women executives experience imposter syndrome in the workplace. *Forbes.* https://www.forbes.com/sites/lucianapaulise/2023/03/08/75-of-women-executives-experience-imposter-syndrome-in-the-workplace/

PlayAblo™ LMS. (2023, September 11). Strong Leadership Networking Skills: 4 tips on building them. *PlayAblo™ LMS Blog.* https://www.playablo.com/CorporateLearning/Blog/networking-skills/

Psychology Today (Ed.). (n.d.). *Confidence.* Psychology Today. https://www.psychologytoday.com/us/basics/confidence

Sanok, J. (2022, April 14). *A guide to setting better boundaries.* Harvard Business Review. https://hbr.org/2022/04/a-guide-to-setting-better-boundaries

Simply Psychology. (2024, January 24). *Maslow's Hierarchy of Needs.* https://www.simplypsychology.org/maslow.html

Suessmuth Dyckerhoff, C., Wang, J., & Wang, J. (n.d.). *Women Matter: An Asian perspective: Harnessing female talent to raise corporate performance.* Mckinsey & Company.

The secrets of successful female networkers. (2020, November 25). Harvard Business Review. https://hbr.org/2019/11/the-secrets-of-successful-female-networkers

Woolf, J. *Understanding Work-Life Balance: What it is (And isn't).* (n.d.). https://www.betterup.com/blog/work-life-balance

Valcour, M. (2014, February 18). *Make your career a success by your own measure.* Harvard Business Review. https://hbr.org/2014/02/make-your-career-a-success-by-your-own-measure

Warren, M. (n.d.). *Why women need male allies in the workplace – and why fighting everyday sexism enriches men too.* The Conversation. https://theconversation.com/

why-women-need-male-allies-in-the-workplace-and-why-fighting-everyday-sexism-enriches-men-too-164384

Woetzel, L., Madgavkar, A., Ellingrud, K., Labaye, E., Devillard, S., Kutcher, E., Manyika, J., Dobbs, R., & Krishnan, M. (2015, September 1). How advancing women's equality can add $12 trillion to global growth. *McKinsey & Company*. https://www.mckinsey.com/featured-insights/employment-and-growth/how-advancing-womens-equality-can-add-12-trillion-to-global-growth

Woetzel, L., Madgavkar, A., Sneader, K., Tonby, O., Lin, D., Lydon, J., Sha, S., Krishnan, M., Ellingrud, K., & Gubieski, M. (2018, April 23). The power of parity: Advancing women's equality in Asia Pacific. *McKinsey & Company*. https://www.mckinsey.com/featured-insights/gender-equality/the-power-of-parity-advancing-womens-equality-in-asia-pacific#part1

Women Don't Self-Promote, But Maybe They Should - Professional & Executive Development | Harvard DCE. Professional & Executive Development | Harvard DCE. https://professional.dce.harvard.edu/blog/women-dont-self-promote-but-maybe-they-should/

Zigarmi, L., Diamond, J., & Mones, L. (2022, January 25). *How women can get comfortable "Playing politics" at work.* Harvard Business Review. https://hbr.org/2022/01/how-women-can-get-comfortable-playing-politics-at-work